Positive Dog Training 101

The Practical Guide to Training Your Dog the Loving and Friendly Way Without Causing your Dog Stress or Harm Using Positive Reinforcement

Table of Contents

Introduction 6

Training with Love 8

   THE POWER OF REINFORCEMENT 9

      How Does it Work? 10

      Positive vs Negative Reinforcement 13

      It's All in the Timing 18

      The Benefits 19

   THE SCIENCE BEHIND POSITIVE REINFORCEMENT 21

Reinforcing Proper Behavior 27

House training an Older Dog 31

   GETTING READY 32

   CRATE TRAINING (IN 1 WEEKEND) 34

   GOING POTTY 44

   PAPER TRAINING 50

Teaching Behavior in 4 Weeks 55

   WHERE TO TRAIN BUDDY? 56

   THE BASIC FORMULA 58

   WEEK 1 TRAINING 61

- What's Your Name? 62
- Teaching Him to Sit 67
- Come Happens 71
- Down! 78

WEEK 2 TRAINING 84
- Stand! 84
- Wait a Second 87
- No Pulling, Mister! 92
- The Touch 99

WEEK 3 TRAINING 103
- Walk Nicely by My Side 104
- Down from a Distance 113
- Stay Longer 118
- Relax! 125

WEEK 4 TRAINING 128
- Take It! 129
- Give! 134
- Leave It! 137
- Go to Your Place 145

Dealing with Misbehavior 151

EXCESSIVE BARKING 151
- Request Barking 152

    Alarm Barking 156
  DISCOURAGING JUMPING UP 158
    The On-Leash Exercise 159
    The Off-Leash Exercise 162
    Jumping Up on Guests 163
  NO BEGGING, PLEASE 166
  STOP LICKING ME... OR YOURSELF 170
  STOPPING SUBMISSIVE WETTING 174

Fun Games for Practice and Bonding 180

  HIGH-FIVE 181
  ROLL OVER 185
  TUG 188
  PLAY DEAD 191
  BELLY CRAWL 194
  TAKE A BOW 195

Phasing Out the Treats 199

  THE FOOD LURES 200
  THE FOOD REWARDS 202

Addressing Anxiety Correctly 206

Bonus Chapter: Agility Training 216

Conclusion 223

Introduction

Whether you have just adopted an older dog and are looking for a way to set some boundaries or it was your lack of commitment that made you skip the puppy training phase – do not worry – training an adult dog who already has established a certain way of doing things is indeed possible.

Stcp away from the traditional way of training and enter the rewarding world of positive reinforcement. Give your dog a reason to behave, and he will! Filled with positive and loving training techniques that will not only teach behavior in just 4 weeks but also form a strong and lasting dog-owner bond, this book will help you prepare your furry friend for his canine citizenship and enjoy hassle-free long walks in the park, filled with fun games, joy, and love.

It doesn't matter if you are dealing with a stubborn, fearful, or an already-trained dog. This guide can not only help you start the training from scratch, but it will also give you amazing ideas on how to continue practicing good behavior and instilling discipline so that your dog will maintain his good manners.

From a four weeks' worth of training plan and the best house training techniques, to the best ways to put a stop to misbehavior problems, teach fun and enjoyable games, as well as keep Buddy fit with agility training, turning your adult Buddy into the most well-behaved ball of fur requires nothing more than the content in this book. And the yummy freeze-dried liver, of course.

Training with Love

They say that dogs are man's best friend. That there is a true and meaningful emotional connection between the canine and its human owner. But even though experts confirm that the human-dog bond is positive and everlasting, it is pretty impossible to believe that you are Buddy's most important thing in the world when your huge ball of fur makes chewed-up shoes, torn-up belongings, and being-woken-up-by-excessive-barking just a part of your day-to-day living. Can you really bring order back to your house?

Mention that you have a disobedient dog to trainers that have been doing their jobs for 20+ years, and you will most likely get the same answer – the choke-chain training method is the only way to go. But is physically forcing your dog to listen to you really the right way to form a loving dog-owner relationship?

Do you force your partner to love you as well? No, you lay out the foundation of a strong relationship with love and understanding. So why should training your dog be any different?

If you think that the positive dog training method is just one of those fads and crazes that modern society has come up with, you couldn't be more wrong. Teaching your dog good behavior while showing him love and respect has proven to be the most effective. If having a partner for life was the reason you adopted Buddy in the first place, then reinforcing his behavior in a positive way is definitely what you should do in order to instill discipline.

The Power of Reinforcement

If you are considering training your dog in a positive way, then you have to understand what the most important training tool – *the reinforcement* – really means.

Although the term 'reinforcement' is often mistakenly used by traditional trainers as a way of punishing your dog, the truth is, reinforcing your pet represents the contrary of punishment. So, if punishing your dog would mean decreasing the dog's behavior, reinforcing him would mean the opposite, or increasing the desired behaviors.

To put it simply, if you purposefully reinforce the actions your dog does, he will be encouraged to do them more often, which is why reinforcement is such a huge help in the dog training process.

How Does it Work?

It all sounds very simple, but how does reinforcement really work? It works by assigning consequences to different actions. Because that's how every living creature learns, really. Through the consequences of their behavior.

That also applies to your dog. Your Buddy is able to store a memory of the outcomes of his actions, and allocate that memory as *good, bad*, or in some cases, *indifferent*. When he thinks a certain action will provide him a good consequence, he is encouraged to perform that action in order to reap the benefits. Similarly, when he finds that some behavior will most likely result in a bad (or indifferent) result, his brain will automatically discourage him from performing that action.

To train your dog to be disciplined and polite, you will have to help him associate good behavior with good consequences in order for him to be encouraged to perform them again in the future. It sounds very simple, I know, but in reality, it is somewhat trickier than that.

Reinforcement is the most helpful training tool, that is true, but it is also a double-edged sword.

Why? Because reinforcement isn't only created by you. It can also be discovered by accident.

For instance, if there is always food available on your kitchen island that Buddy can steal, he will learn that jumping up onto tables is a behavior that is rewarding and, therefore, should be repeated. Now, you may think this is simply an act of disobedience, but here, the truth is that Buddy was simply encouraged to learn this behavior. Your dog cannot really differentiate the behaviors he learns by accident from those that you train him to understand. His brain works in a simple way – repeat what is beneficial to you.

With positive training, you can encourage the desired actions, as well as discourage the ones that are not.

Positive vs Negative Reinforcement

When it comes to training with reinforcement, there are two distinctive types here: positive and negative. But although the first thing that comes to mind when mentioning positive and negative is good and bad, the truth is, positive and negative reinforcement do not represent the nice and the nasty. Their origin can be found in mathematics.

Positive and negative reinforcement means *adding* and *taking away* something. They are not good and bad, and they surely cannot be classified as rewarding and punishing. Why? Because there are no punishments in training with reinforcement. So what do they mean?

Positive Reinforcement– Positive reinforcement means adding something in order to increase (or reinforce) the dog's desired behavior. The most popular – and most convenient – way of reinforcing the dog's actions is by giving him rewards. For instance, giving Buddy a biscuit for taking a seat.

That's called positive reinforcement because the dog finds the added reward pleasant. The goal here is for the dog to associate the behavior with the reward, so he can be encouraged to repeat the same action again in the future, with the purpose of getting the tasty treat again, of course.

But even though the food rewards are the most common, you can also reinforce the dog's behavior by giving him attention, playing a fun game with him, granting access to someplace he enjoys being at, etc.

Negative Reinforcement – Negative reinforcement, on the other hand, means the opposite of adding. It means subtracting something, but even though most mistakenly confuse this term with taking away some things that the dog finds pleasant in order to punish or correct, negative reinforcement actually takes away the things that the dog finds unpleasant.

For instance, the trainer applies pressure to get the dog into a sitting position and then takes away the physical discomfort by releasing the force, when the dog is already sitting down and, therefore, carries out the desired action.

Negative and positive reinforcements do not go hand in hand, and you will not find a dog trainer that uses them both. We are discussing the negative reinforcement now in order to understand that this term does not represent correcting or punishing your dog, as can be found on many dog websites and blogs.

So, How Do You Correct a Behavior?

Where there is reinforcement, there are no punishments. However, despite the fact that you will be training your dog with the most positive and pleasant methods, there will be times when you will simply have to intervene.

For instance, if your pup refuses to come to you when out in the park, and he decides that playing with his ball is way more fun than walking at heel, you will obviously need to do something in order to let him know that his behavior is unacceptable. Here, the best tactic is to simply take away his ball. This is punishment, yes. But the time when the punishment occurs is of great significance.

If you feel that there is a strong need for you to take a toy away from your dog at the beginning of the training, then, by all means, do it. But know that positive reinforcement and punishments do not go hand in hand because once the dog is trained, there is no need to correct his behavior. A trained dog is supposed to come to you when called, not refuse to cooperate. You may find it necessary to yell

"No" or take his toy away from him at the beginning of the training, while your dog is still disobedient.

Once you train your dog with positive reinforcement, he will be able to perform the desired actions with ease. The only way to correct a behavior is with training. You can train Buddy to let go of his misbehavior with positive reinforcement as well, which we will discuss in more detail later in this book.

To sum up, you can sometimes decide on a humane punishment such as taking a toy away or not allowing access to an area, but only while still in the process of training. Just keep in mind that by taking his toy away, you are not teaching Buddy a lesson. You cannot create new behaviors with punishments. It's impossible, and it will only contribute to decreased cooperation out of the fear of receiving punishment.

Once your dog masters the basic commands and is ready to learn new behaviors, you should avoid empty punishments, but strive to teach good behavior so that Buddy can learn how to properly behave, permanently. By incorporating positive reinforcement techniques, you help your dog understand what is asked of him and repeat the good behavior in the long term.

It's All in the Timing

If you poke a bear with a stick, the animal will get angry and ready to attack right there and right then. The bear will not leave for a few minutes to think about it and then come back later to finish its job. Your action will have immediate consequences.

We've all evolved to learn that way, and so has your dog. You can only teach him decent behavior if you reward the desired action immediately after it has happened. It's no use treating your dog for sitting down a few minutes after he puts his bottom on the floor. Buddy can associate the reward with the action only if he is given the treat immediately after performing it.

So, if you want to train your dog the right way, you need to understand that it's all in the timing. Praise and reward should be given to Buddy the second he has completed the desired actions. Otherwise, he will never be able to truly understand why he is getting all the rewards, and you will never be able to train him properly.

The Benefits

The best thing about positive reinforcement is that it allows you to teach your dog good behavior in a positive and humane way while keeping his confidence up at the same time. Dog owners who use this training method report fewer behavioral problems than those who choose more traditional training techniques. Getting your dog to behave on a day-to-day basis is most effective if the dog sees something in it for him as well.

But besides it being super effective, positive reinforcement comes with a set of other benefits as well. Some of them are:

- Positive reinforcement trains Buddy toward good behavior, rather than only toward responses.

- The training is an enjoyable and fun experience for both you and your dog, and unlike the traditional methods, it feels less of a task.

- It helps you build a healthy and strong bond between you and Buddy.

- It will improve your communication with your dog.

- Every member of your family can be involved in the training process; you are not the only person in charge.

- It can be a great exercise for your dog, allowing Buddy to burn off tons of energy.

- It can be used for many behavioral issues. For instance, if you have an aggressive dog, punishing him traditionally may make the situation worse. Positive reinforcement can help you find the perfect way to correct misbehavior and instill proper habits.

The Science Behind Positive Reinforcement

Over the last couple of decades, there has been a serious shift towards less punitive dog training techniques. Today, the words 'dominance,' 'respect,' and 'pack leader' have very little meaning in the process of training. If you observe a modern trainer teaching dogs simple commands, you will see how different and more humane they are than those old school dog lessons that our parents (and some of us – no need to beat yourself up over it) were used to in the past.

But even though there are more and more positive dog trainers, there are still those who look at positive reinforcement as nothing but a way of creating spoiled dogs. If you, too, are wondering whether all those rewards, treats, and smooches will only contribute to Buddy becoming addicted to them and will eventually turn to naughtiness only to get them, you cannot be more wrong.

Positive and permissive are two very different things. You are training with positivity, and although it may look like you are pleading with your dog and begging him to perform a simple task, that's far from the truth. Positive reinforcement may depend on luring your dog into participating in the process, but that's only short-term. The reward is a great encouragement tool that will help your dog to be more involved and learn sooner. Once he adopts proper habits, the rewards will be phased out.

Those who best understand this are, perhaps, those people who have already made the shift from traditional to positive and have experienced both worlds first-hand. If you are not one of those people or don't know anyone who can vouch for the efficiency of this method, then perhaps the multiple studies and scientific results will be convincing enough for you to give positive reinforcement a try.

Dominance is Outdated

A study published by the Clinical Veterinary Sciences under the University of Bristol has found that the aggression in dogs has nothing to do with them trying to assert dominance over their owners.

By spending over 6 months studying freely-interacting dogs, the researchers found that dogs are not motivated to keep their place in the pack's order, as many trainers think. In fact, these academics say that 'dominance decreasing' techniques are not only worthless, but they can also be dangerous and worsen the canine's behavior.

Punishment Leads to Disobedience

In the "Applied Animal Behaviour Science" journal from 2010, there is published a study that shows the correlation between the dog's behavior, the inconsistent level of the owner's engagement in activities, and regular punishments. The analysis of 1276 Quaternary helped the researchers conclude that regular use of punishments only increases excitability and anxiety in dogs while using rewards can calm and distract the canine.

This study also concluded that not engaging in regular activities with the dog can also lead to behavioral problems. It's easy to understand that reward-based training can decrease the misbehavior and knock down fear-related anxiety and aggression.

Positive Reinforcements Instead of Positive Punishments and Negative Reinforcements

A study from 217, published in the "Journal of Veterinary Behavior," has concluded that aversive training methods such as training with negative reinforcements or using positive punishments can have a significant negative impact on the dog's physical and mental health.

The study has found that even though positive punishments can be effective to some extent, they are not more beneficial than the positive reinforcements training method. In fact, the evidence showed that it is quite the opposite. Dog owners should train their dogs with positive reinforcements instead of positive punishments or negative reinforcements, in order to instill disobedience and maintain the welfare state of their dog.

Reinforcing Proper Behavior

Think of training as a two-way street. It is not just you who has to give 100 percent; your dog is just as involved in the process as you are. It doesn't seem so in the beginning, because you don't start off as the trainer, but the student. Yes, you've read it correctly. You are the S T U D E N T. How? Because Buddy is already used to training you. Most of you probably think that I am talking nonsense, but if you give it some thought, you will see that I am, in fact, right.

Dogs know what is to their advantage and what's not – it is a skill that they have used since the day they were born. And they don't think twice about getting what they want. In fact, everything they do is about getting what they want. Take begging at the table, for example. Buddy will beg and whine, and touch you with his nose and paws, until you give up and give him a slice of meat. Or think about this scenario. You are sitting on the couch watching TV when Buddy decides to drop a ball in your lap. You instantly pick up the ball and throw it to your dog. See? He has indeed trained you well. And there is nothing wrong with that, either. You just have to think about which actions you really want to reinforce. Because after all, the whole point of training is about reinforcing good behavior.

Speaking of reinforcement, here is where your attitude plays a huge part. How you approach the training is of great importance. During training, you need to maintain a positive attitude in order to reinforce the proper behavior and not mistakenly create an aversion towards something. For instance, let's say that you are running late for work and you have to put Buddy in his crate. You call and call for him, but he is nowhere to be found. All of a sudden, he walks into the house through the back door with muddy paws. He has been digging. You are now furious that you will have to be even more late thanks to the fact that you have some wiping and sweeping to do. So, what's your first impression? You give him a good scolding. And, what will be Buddy's thoughts? *He called me, I came, he got angry.* Your dog may have a guilty look on his face, but that is surely not because he understands that he has made a mess. Dogs look guilty because you get angry. And, in this case, by getting angry, you are only contributing to Buddy associating *"Come boy"* with *getting angry and yelling.* Do you think he will come to you next time you call him?

You have to be very careful about your attitude and reactions because they are what creates Buddy's responses. If you want to reinforce the proper behavior, you need to address it directly. If you ask your dog to come, you cannot start yelling about the fact that he made a mess.

Instead, you praise him for coming to you. If you catch him in the act of digging, only in that case can you let him know that he is behaving badly. In that instance. Not a minute later when the digging frenzy passes. Otherwise, Buddy cannot really know what you are truly mad about, can he?

House training an Older Dog

Before you jump straight to teaching Buddy *high-fives* or other fun games so that you can show off your training skills, you need to first prevent your house from becoming an unsanitary environment. And while it is true that house training a puppy is much easier than training an adult dog to go potty, that does not mean that you cannot teach your furry friend where to eliminate waste.

Although it is in their nature not to soil their quarters, dogs that haven't been trained (or haven't been trained successfully) may have established bad habits. In order to break this behavior, you need to go back to the basics, assess the situation, instill healthy habits, and most importantly, be patient.

Getting Ready

Before you try to teach Buddy his new drop zone, you have a few things that you need to take care of, first:

Do a Background Check

If you have adopted your dog just recently, then a background check is indeed in order. You need to find out as much as you can about Buddy's previous upbringing so you can know exactly what you are dealing with and which issues you need to overcome before starting the house training process. Perhaps Buddy was partially house trained in the past. Maybe he was confined for long periods of time on a concrete floor. Maybe he wasn't allowed access to the indoors. There might be some surface preferences for elimination that you need to reset in order to help Buddy get used to the new environment.

Talk to Your Veterinarian

Whether your dog was house trained and has just started eliminating waste in the house or he has bad habits that you need to pull by the root, it is really important to talk to your vet first in order to rule out some underlying medical conditions. You may think that your dog is just stubborn, but he might be dealing with kidney problems or just has an upset tummy due to recent diet changes.

Pay Attention to Buddy's Elimination Habits

In order for you to avoid elimination problems in the future, you first need to know when and where they happen. For instance, if Buddy urinates only on ceramic tiles, you can restrict his access to those rooms, or you can cover the tiles with rugs or towels in order to discourage elimination there so you can start house training and teaching your habits.

Keep Your Home Clean

If your dog is used to having home accidents, then you need to frequently and thoroughly clean the waste odors not only so you can maintain the home hygiene, but also to prevent the odor from encouraging Buddy to eliminate indoors. It is best to try an enzymatic cleaner for this purpose, as they have been known to successfully destroy odors from pet waste. Make sure to also check places that aren't easily reachable such as closets, under the bed, behind the door, etc.

Crate Training (in 1 Weekend)

Before you start the potty-training process, it is important for your dog to be crate trained first. Most dogs are prone to having accidents when left alone. In order to prevent that from happening, the best approach is to confine Buddy to a smaller space when you are not around. And since dogs do not like to soil the place where they sleep and eat, crate training can lay out the perfect foundation for self-control. It's simple really – if Buddy cannot get to the place where he feels free to make a mess, he will be encouraged to 'hold it in.'

Although it sounds like a long and overwhelming process, getting your dog used to the crate can actually be done in a single weekend, which is a great opportunity for busy workers to embark on the dog training train.

The very first thing you need to do is to get the crate ready. Assuming you have already purchased a proper crate that fits your dog's needs, place it in a location that works for you both. If necessary, place some towels or a mat inside to make sure Buddy will be comfortable. Leave the door of the crate open and let Buddy explore.

Then, follow these steps:

Step 1

Friday afternoon, place a couple of doggy treats in the crate. Let them sit there for Buddy to discover. If Buddy enters the crate willingly, mark the behavior the second he steps inside and let him have the reward. If your dog is afraid of getting inside the crate, do not force him to. The worst thing that could happen is for your dog to develop negative feelings toward the crate.

Step 2

Friday night, serve Buddy's dinner in the crate, but make sure to place his bowl closer to the door, not the back of the crate. When Buddy starts eating, start gradually sliding the bowl a bit further into the crate. If he doesn't like to enter completely, give him a few minutes to change his mind. If he loses interest in his dinner, return the bowl a bit closer to the door, but where he still needs to at least place his head inside.

Do not forget to give him a reward after dinner.

Step 3

Saturday morning, start with a more active training. Stand next to his crate and call Buddy. Let Buddy sniff a truly irresistible treat but do not let him have it just yet. Throw the treat inside the crate and wait for his reaction. If he steps inside, immediately say a verbal cue such as **"Bed"** or **"Kennel,"** then mark the behavior and give him another treat.

Repeat this about a dozen times, gradually placing the treat further inside the crate. When Buddy enters the crate completely, give him another treat while he is still there. Then another one. And yet another treat. Finally, top the rewarding with his favorite toy. The point is for Buddy to spend a couple of minutes inside. Then give him a release cue and give him another treat outside of the crate.

Step 4

Later in the morning, repeat the session, only this time, give him the verbal cue before throwing the treat inside. Say **"Kennel"** or whatever word you are using, and with the treat hand, show him the crate. If Buddy goes inside on his own, give him the treat inside and gently close the door. As soon as he eats the treat, let him out.

Repeat this a few times, gradually increasing the length of the time Buddy spends inside with the door closed.

If he is anxious, close the door part way. Make sure to stay positive and to give the verbal cue with an upbeat and cheerful voice.

If Buddy doesn't enter the crate willingly, repeat the previous exercise one more time.

Step 5

Around noon, repeat the same process. Keep increasing the duration until Buddy is comfortable to spend a whole minute inside.

Step 6

Saturday evening, you should start leaving your Bud alone in the crate. Of course, you should try with short periods of time and gradually increase the length. First, practice a few short stays in the crate, with the door closed. Then, close the door and take a couple of steps back. Then take a walk around the room. Do NOT leave the room at this point. Repeat this process about a dozen times. Step away from the crate but make sure that Buddy can still see you.

Step 7

Sunday morning, it is time for longer stays. Ask your dog to go inside the crate and give him something that will keep boredom at bay. His favorite chew toy will do the job. Close the door and let Buddy stay inside the crate for about half an hour or so. Again, do NOT leave the room just yet. Relax on the couch, watch TV, read a book, whatever you do, just don't leave the room. After 30 minutes, give Buddy the release word and let him out. An hour later, repeat the same process.

Tip: Do not lavish Buddy with rewards when he gets out of the crate. Remember, you are training him to love spending time inside the crate, not to be encouraged to get out.

Step 8

In order to make sure that your dog will not get anxious when you leave him alone in the crate and walk out of the room, the best tactic is to make sure that Buddy is tired and will probably need rest. Around noon, give him a really good workout.

Go out for a long walk, play *chase me* in the backyard, go running with Buddy... The point is for your dog to have a long play session so that he can get tired.

Step 9

Give Buddy the cue to go inside the crate, give him a toy he can chew on, and close the door of the crate. Then, leave the room and do not check on Buddy for 10 whole minutes. After ten minutes, go back to the room and use the release word to get Buddy out of the crate. After 10 minutes, repeat the same process. Only this time, leave the room for 15-20 minutes. Repeat this process until you gradually build up to leaving Buddy alone in the crate for a whole hour.

Make sure to give your dog the chance to go potty in between and use the breaks to play and cuddle with your ball of fur to keep anxiety at bay.

Step 10

Early in the evening, it is time for you to actually leave the house. Give buddy the verbal cue to go inside the crate and close the door. Make sure to provide an appropriate chew toy. Then, leave the house and don't go in for 10 minutes. When you get back, let Buddy out, but do not reward or celebrate the fact that he has come out of the crate. After 30 minutes, repeat this again, only this time, leave Buddy in the crate for 20 minutes. Use the release word, open the door, and then go about your evening. Nothing exciting has happened.

Step 11

Early on Monday morning, give Buddy a good workout and make sure he gets tired. Get ready for work, then give him the verbal cue to go inside the crate. Again, make sure to provide a proper chew toy to keep him busy. Then head out, but don't make a fuss about your departure. Make sure to return after a few hours to take Buddy for his midday walk. If your work doesn't allow you to take such a break (or if none of the family members can take Buddy out), then hiring a dog walker is definitely a must. Keep in mind that an adult dog should be left alone in the crate for about 4 hours, but Buddy should absolutely NEVER spend more than 6 hours alone in the crate.

After the weekend training, most dogs should handle well spending a few hours alone in the crate. If you think that your dog is overly anxious, consult with your veterinarian.

Going Potty

With a puppy, you have a blank slate. It is you who sets the foundation for good behavior, so you can say that it is easy to teach him to go potty. With an adult dog, things are different. Older dogs have already established elimination habits. Your job is to rewrite that chapter and help them adopt healthier habits. And while that seems like a lot of work, the good thing about teaching a dog to go potty is that adult dogs learn quickly. Most older dogs can be potty trained in less than a week.

Make the Time

Dogs learn quickly, yes, but it is you who has to find the time for training. It is best if you could take a few days off work so you can focus on the training process. The routine here is of extreme importance, so make sure to provide consistency.

Establish the Area

Your dog needs to have a specific drop zone where he can eliminate waste. It is highly recommended that his drop zone is outdoors, but not too far from your home so you can conveniently take him there every time he needs to go.

If you live in a house and have a backyard, then you can designate a special area in your yard for this purpose. If you live in a high-rise apartment or if you are unable to provide outdoor access that easily, in that case, paper training your dog is recommended.

Escort!

If you have a backyard and your dog was partially potty trained, then you are probably used to just opening the door and letting him go outside to do his business. To retrain him properly, you have to actually take him there yourself. If your dog was not house trained at all before, even better. Just make sure to escort him to the designated spot, on a leash.

Use the Verbal Cue

Once you are at the desired elimination zone, wait for Buddy to do his business. Pay attention to his movements and the second you see him urinating or defecating, say **"Go Potty"** or whatever cue works best for you. Immediately after Buddy is done, reward him with a yummy treat.

Repeat this every time he goes potty, for as long as it takes for him to go on cue whenever you are at the drop zone (assuming that you already know his potty schedule well and that you are sure he actually needs to go, of course).

Rely on Consistency

The key to successful house training lies in having a consistent feeding and potty routine.

It is pretty simple, really. The more regular his feeding is, the more regular Buddy will eliminate waste. Be consistent with his feeding times, as well as the amount of food that is recommended for his age and/or unique medical condition. Consult with your vet and stick to that schedule.

Once you establish consistent feeding, it will be much easier for you to pinpoint when Buddy will feel the urge to eliminate. Most healthy dogs need to go every few hours, but after a couple of days of consistent feeding, you will be able to find out when those times are so you can take Buddy out then, in order to avoid accidents.

Avoid Accidents

The goal is for Buddy to have as few accidents at home as possible. Of course, you can prevent this with a consistent routine, but it is impossible to strictly plan his physiological needs. Pay attention to signs that Buddy needs to go. Most dogs start circling and whining when they have the need to go, so if you see that or if your dog suddenly starts sniffing and pacing, then attach his leash and immediately take him to his drop zone outside.

Also, make sure to put away his water bowl before bedtime so that you can prevent him from urinating at home during the night. Don't worry. If Buddy is really thirsty, he will let you know. This is obviously not recommended if Buddy had a lot of exercise at night or if it is too hot at home.

Do NOT Punish

If you see that Buddy has made an accident, do not yell at him or punish him in any way. The old fashioned newspaper roll is not only cruel and inhumane but highly ineffective as well. Clean the accident and follow the tips from above to prevent it from happening again.

If you, however, catch Buddy during the act, midstream, just clap your hand or say a negative word such as **"Oops"** in order to startle him. Then put on his leash and take him to his drop zone. Say **"Go Potty"** and wait for him to do his business there. Once he eliminates, reward the good behavior.

Even if Buddy doesn't have the need to go anymore, it is still beneficial to take him outside to the elimination spot so he can see the connection between the *"Oops"* with the *"Go Potty"* and his drop zone, in order to understand that he has made a mistake.

What If Buddy Takes Forever to Go?

If Buddy needs a lot of time to go every time he is taken to the drop zone, it is probably because he is *hanging on*. Most dogs do that after they associate the *"Go Potty"* with being returned home. Do not take him straight home after he has done his business. Reward him and praise him like crazy, then spend some time playing with him outside or take him for a walk. Repeat this for a couple of days and soon enough, Buddy will start going on cue as he will be keen to go potty thanks to the fact that it results with treats and games.

Keep in Mind: Old dogs need to eliminate waste more frequently than younger, healthier dogs. That is not a result of unsuccessful training but happens because Buddy cannot hold the waste as long. If that is the case, you might want to consider providing a place inside your home where Buddy can go potty when you are not home or engage a neighbor that can help out.

Paper Training

To paper train your dog means to teach him to eliminate waste on a small, designated spot in your home, that is covered with a special pad, mat, or even a pile of newspapers. This is not recommended for healthy dogs and owners that have the ability to provide a consistent potty routine outside. However, if you live in a high-rise apartment downtown, if you have a very busy schedule, if Buddy has difficulty going outside, or if you are in no condition to get your dog there, then paper training can be of great benefit to you and your furry friend.

Select the Potty Area

The very first thing you need to do is to choose a potty area inside your home that works for you. Give this a good thought as you will be training your dog to go potty there, permanently. So, where are you comfortable for Buddy to eliminate waste? Think about it well. The tile floor in the kitchen may be the easiest to clean, but do you really want Buddy to be soiling this area? Keep in mind that Buddy will have to be confined to this area while you are not home, so choose wisely.

Line the Area

Line the area where you want Buddy to eliminate waste with special puppy pads, a mat that can soak up the urine, or even by arranging a pile of newspapers there. Choose whatever works for you and what you can afford, but keep in mind that special puppy pads are more absorbent and leave almost no mess behind.

Just make sure to provide a lot of space in the beginning, so that Buddy can associate the pads with his urge to eliminate waste.

Encourage Buddy to Use Them

Around his potty times, place Buddy on top of the pads and wait for him to eliminate. The instant he starts doing that, say **"Pad"** or **"Potty"** or whatever cue you want to use. Once he is done, reward him. Repeat this for as long as it takes for him to learn that he should do his business on the pads.

If Buddy doesn't want to step onto the pads, physically place him there or lure him onto the pads with a yummy treat.

Reduce

Once Buddy begins eliminating waste onto the lined area, you will have to start gradually reducing the size of it. You wouldn't want your Buddy to use half of your room as a drop zone now, would you? Most owners are comfortable with their dog eliminating waste in a small area in some corner of their house (just like a litter box for cats), so ideally, you should aim for that.

Each day, reduce the size by a 1/8 or so until you get to a suitable size.

Encourage Some More

You need to continue encouraging Buddy to use that area, even if he is confused. At first, he might just try to eliminate where those pads used to be. If you catch him trying to eliminate outside of that area, say **"Oops"** and clap your hands. Then immediately take Buddy to the area and give him the verbal cue **"Potty"** or **"Pad."** Keep rewarding and praising the good behavior to encourage him to repeat it.

What If Buddy is Struggling?

Keep in mind that dogs progress differently. If you see that Buddy is seriously struggling, take a step back. Increase the area by a ¼ and let Buddy get more comfortable with eliminating waste there. Give it some more time and then reduce again.

Teaching Behavior in 4 Weeks

In order for your dog to start listening to you, you first have to teach him your language. Doing so will not only result in mutual understanding but it will also be a great opportunity for you to become a bit more fluent in Buddy's language, as well. Being able to easily understand each others needs and wants will take your communication and connection to a higher level, which will, in turn, enable you to embark on a fun adventure that will empower you both equally.

This chapter represents the core of this book as it contains the mechanics of an effective dog training program. In theory, the content of this chapter represents about 4 weeks' worth of training. However, don't be disappointed if you cannot convince Buddy to get off your couch in time for the next session. The four-week plan is really just a plan. Nothing is set in stone, so feel free to take as much time as you need, or even fast-forward if your dog is a canine prodigy. The main point of this chapter is not to obsess over getting your dog to behave in less than a month but to lay out the foundation for Buddy's future.

Where to Train Buddy?

Many new dog owners think that the nearest park will be the perfect place for them to start training their dogs. But what they don't know is that going outside immediately sets them on the path to failure. If your dog hasn't been able to learn proper manners for whatever reason and is used to doing whatever pleases him, you will have a pretty hard time taming him when he gets wired up by outer distractions. Keep in mind that you should take baby steps and start from the very beginning. Your dog probably doesn't even respond to his own name yet; what makes you think that you can handle the presence of other dogs, bikes passing through, birds, squirrels, and all that outdoor noise? The best place to start training Buddy is inside the house.

Start the training inside and make sure to do it when there are minimal distractions. For instance, if you have a hyperactive toddler jumping around the house, do the training when he is taking a nap.

If you always use the same room for training, your dog will be less and less distracted and will eventually learn to put his sole focus on you. However, as beneficial as this is for teaching a new behavior, keep in mind that once Buddy learns a skill, you should take it somewhere else. Otherwise, your dog might mistakenly associate the behavior with, for instance, an object in that room. For example, if you do the training in the garage and Buddy is used to sitting down next to your toolbox, giving him the "Sit" command in the living room may not work. He will probably become confused as there will be no toolbox for him to sit down next to. This will most likely make you believe that your dog is stubborn, when in fact, it is a training mistake you are dealing with. Many dog owners make this mistake, so make sure that, once Buddy learns a skill, you start practicing it in different places.

The Basic Formula

Teaching your dog a new behavior requires a simple but consistent formula. This 5-step process will help you instill proper discipline and teach Buddy good manners. Just stick to this rule and success is guaranteed:

1: Get the dog's behavior.

Whether you capture, shape, or lure the behavior, the very first step is to get your Bud to perform the desired behavior.

2: Mark the behavior.

Whether you choose the clicker or you simply tell Buddy "Good boy" immediately after the performed action, marking the behavior is of crucial importance for the training process as it helps the dog instantly get that what he has done is good and that the reward is coming.

3: Give Buddy a reward for the performed action.

The best way to get your dog to learn the desired behavior is to motivate him to repeat it again in the future. By using a yummy treat, favorite toy, granting outdoor access, or some other reward that your dog will enjoy the most, the point is to help him learn that the performed behavior is good and rewarding.

4: Add a verbal cue before the action is performed so that Buddy can associate the command with the correct behavior.

In order for your dog to successfully associate the proper behavior with the right command, you need to give the verbal cue just before the action is performed. For instance, you say "Sit" when you see that Buddy is about to sit down. Asking him to do it when he is not offering the behavior easily may only cause confusion, and worse, you risk teaching him that the word "Sit" means "ignore me and go play with your squeaky toy."

5: Use the verbal command to elicit the appropriate behavior.

Once your dog becomes familiar with the verbal command and its meaning, you can then start using the cue first, in order to elicit the correct action. Just keep in mind that in order for the training to be successful, you need to have Buddy's undivided attention, so make sure that your ball of fur is actually focused on you before starting.

Week 1 Training

Training an adult dog is very different than training a young puppy. You'd think that it's easier since a grown-up dog can perform many different tasks with ease, but the truth is, the older your dog is, the trickier it is for you to direct him in the right way. And, if your dog is used to getting things his way, training him can sound like an especially daunting chore to you. However, if you start things from the very beginning, even the most stubborn ball of fur can learn proper behavior in less than a month.

The first week should be for the most basic commands and simple behavior. Do not try to tackle more advanced training programs because your dog already knows how to sit. If Buddy hasn't had a training class in his life, all of this can be new to him. In order to keep him interested, you have to avoid asking too much in return. Just follow this carefully crafted training program and keep his enthusiasm high throughout the process.

What's Your Name?

Knowing his name is the very first thing that your dog has to learn. And I do not mean just for the sake of avoiding an identity crisis. Giving you his full attention whenever you call his name can save you a lot of trouble in the future. The goal of this training exercise is to teach your dog that hearing his name means "drop everything and look at me."

When teaching your older dog his name, the key to success is to say it as often as possible, and not only when you need him to give you his attention, but pretty much every time you talk to him. Just make sure not to get frustrated if your dog needs a little bit more time to master this lesson. This is especially important in case you've adopted an abandoned dog, as he probably needs some extra persuading in order to start cooperating.

Here is how you can name-train your dog:

1. Get ready by ensuring that you are in a distraction-free place where your dog can give you his full attention. Place a couple of tasty treats in your pocket for rewarding.

2. Sit down with your dog and make sure that you have his attention. You can brush him, give him a massage, or just talk to him for a while. The point is for your dog to be focused on you before saying his name out loud.

3. Say his name and mark the behavior. This is best done with a clicker, but you can also mark it with a smooching sound or a clap.

4. Immediately give him the reward.

5. Repeat this process a dozen times. The point is for your Buddy to associate the sound of his name with the reward, in order to remember to look at you whenever he hears you calling him.

6. Now that you've been playing this game for a while, it is time to test your Buddy's attention. Wait until your dog looks away. Then, say his name to check if he has already started associating his name with the reward. Buddy's head should snap back toward your direction when he hears his name. If it does, mark the behavior immediately and give him a treat. If not, practice saying his name when he is focused on you a bit longer before testing him again.

Play a Game!

When your dog begins getting the gist of the exercise, you can pay a game involving all of the members in your family:

1. Give everyone a couple of treats and gather around in a semicircle.

2. Say Buddy's name. When he looks at you, mark the behavior with a clap, a click, or by saying "Good boy," and give him a treat.

3. Have someone else say Buddy's name. Take turns saying his name. Just remember to instantly mark and reward the behavior.

This is a fun way for Buddy to practice and learn the meaning of his name.

What If Buddy Is not Responding?

If your dog doesn't look at you when you say his name, even after spending a decent amount of training, then perhaps you need to make some changes. In most cases, the dog doesn't respond because he is not motivated to play along or because he is preoccupied with something that's more interesting to him. Try to take the training somewhere with fewer distractions and change the reward. For instance, if you're using regular doggy food, treat him with something a bit more tempting. If that doesn't seem to do the trick, then schedule the training before his meals. Training him on an empty stomach may motivate him to play along just to get the treat.

Also, you could try marking the behavior with some exciting sounds like the squeak of his favorite toy. If Buddy is still unresponsive, then perhaps you need to have his hearing checked. But don't worry. Even if your dog is hearing-impaired, there are a lot of different ways for you to mark the behavior. A fun vibrating collar and a light beam are just a couple of great options.

Teaching Him to Sit

"Sit" is the most basic command, and besides their name, usually the first one that dogs master. Besides the fact that getting your dog to sit down can be useful in various situations, mastering this command is also the beginning of establishing a strong bond with Buddy. Make sure to make the session enjoyable.

1. Fill your pockets with tasty treats and go to the designated training area.

2. Hang out there with Buddy and wait until he sits down. When he puts his bottom to the ground, immediately click, or make the marking sound, and give him the treat.

3. Wait for him to sit down again and repeat the process a dozen times.

4. Once your dog begins understanding the connection between the behavior and the treat, you should start eliciting the action with the verbal command.

5. Stand in front of your dog with a treat in your hand. Make sure he notices it so that you'll have his full attention.

6. Place the treat near his nose and gently raise it above his head. Chances are, your dog will keep his eyes locked on the treat and follow it with his nose. Then, lower the treat down to the ground.

7. When you notice that Buddy is about to sit down, give him the **"Sit"** command.

8. Once he is down, mark the good behavior and give him the treat.

9. Repeat this for about 10 minutes or so, but don't push too hard. If you notice your dog looking away or sniffing

around, he is most likely bored. Take a break and resume another time. If you're training consistently, your dog will most likely catch on after only a week.

What If the Dog is Very Active?

If you are dealing with an especially rambunctious dog, then the previous method may not work so well. Dogs that are very active will most likely just jump around at the sight of the treat. Getting them to sit down can be a true challenge. For that purpose, you will probably need to offer physical guidance in order to have better control over Buddy:

1. Put Buddy on a leash. He needs to be able to stay in place in order to give you his attention. By putting him on a leash, you will have him close to your side.

2. Stand next to your dog. You will need to lower him to a sitting position physically, so give Buddy a gentle push above his rear legs.

3. Just before Buddy puts his bottom to the ground, say **"Sit."**

4. Mark the behavior immediately and give him a treat.

5. Repeat this for a day or two, then try the sitting command again, but without using your hand on Buddy's back. The point is for Buddy to associate the command with the behavior and the behavior with the reward.

What If Buddy Refuses to Offer a Sit?

If your dog is not interested in sitting down on cue, you will probably have to spend some more time teaching him the connection between the behavior and the reward.

Whenever you see him sitting down, say "Sit," and immediately give him a treat.

Another thing you can try is to practice the sit command when your dog is a bit tired. Go for a walk or play a game of fetch before the training session in order to get him pooped and encourage him to sit down.

Come Happens

Most dog trainers agree that "Come" is one of the most important commands that your dog has to master. Also known as *recall*, "come" will give your dog the freedom to walk off-leash and provide him with endless exploring opportunities to shake off that extra energy. Mastering this technique will give you peace of mind that your dog will come to you when called, which will be of enormous importance when Buddy decides that chasing a squirrel across the road is a fun way to spend the afternoon.

But, before we start with the steps to teaching him this command, it is important to mention that you should pay attention not to *poison the cue*. You cannot be teaching Buddy to come to you when called and give him rewards for it and then tell him to go away when he comes to you while you are trying to take an afternoon nap. In order for Buddy to truly master the "Come" command, you need to make him feel that coming to you is something positive and rewarding. Never punish him for coming to you just because you are not in the mood for it.

Also, do not use the "Come" command when you want to cut the walk short, clip his nails, give him a bath, or do something that Buddy doesn't enjoy. You need to help him associate "Come" with positivity, not with the fact that his play time might be over.

Here are simple instructions that will teach your Bud to come to you in no time:

1. Fill your pockets with treats and get your dog in the same room as you. Stand near him, then turn and run away from him.

2. If Buddy starts running towards you, say **"Come"** immediately, then mark the behavior and give your dog the treat when he approaches you. If he isn't too excited to make a move, see if you can encourage him to follow you by making a smooching noise or squeaking a toy. The point is to get Buddy excited in order to follow you.

3. Once Buddy starts running to you every time you give him the command, you should decrease your movement and get him to come to you even when you are standing still.

4. Do not take "Come" outside just yet. If you are not at least 90 percent sure that

Buddy will come to you when called, it is way too early for you to take him off the leash. Practice this command inside your house or in the comfort of your backyard for as long as it takes for Buddy to understand that hearing the word "come" means to come to you willingly.

What If Buddy Isn't Interested in Following You?

If you are dealing with a very unenthusiastic dog, then it is possible that your ball of fur will lose interest in following you after the first couple attempts. If that happens, do not despair. You just have to start the training at a much slower pace; that's it. If Buddy isn't particularly excited to come to you willingly, then the best way to train him on this command is while he is on the leash.

1. Leash Buddy. In order for you to keep him close and make sure that he is focused on you, attach a shorter leash to his collar.

2. Grab some doggy treats, pick up the leash and stand just a couple of steps away from your dog.

3. Show him the treat as you take a step backward. Start taking backward steps and wait for Buddy to come your way. When he starts following you, say **"Come."**

4. Keep moving backward slowly, until your dog reaches you. When that happens, immediately mark the behavior, give him the reward, and praise him like crazy.

5. Do this a couple of times, then reduce the distance to a single step backward.

The goal is to be able to get Buddy to come to you without taking any steps. When that happens, you can start practicing this command off the leash.

Keep it Fun!

In order to teach your dog that "*come*" is a positive thing, you need to help him associate the command with excitement. And the best way to do so is to make sure that the training sessions are fun and enjoyable for him.

Round-Robin. Once Buddy begins responding to the "*come*" command successfully, you can add an extra dash of complexity by playing a fun and challenging game. Invite 2-3 friends or family members to stand in a circle, about twenty feet apart from each other. Give them a few small treats and let each of them issue the "*come*" command. When Buddy comes to them, let them mark the behavior and give him the treat.

<u>Hide and Seek.</u> Practicing the "*come*" command regularly, even if Buddy comes to you willingly, is of great importance. To keep it fun, set aside 10 minutes to play hide and seek with your dog every once in a while. After Buddy has mastered the skill, hide in another room and issue the command. Let Buddy find you and come to you. Once he does that, lavish him with treats and praises.

What If Buddy Isn't Cooperative at All?

If you have adopted an older dog and have trouble teaching him the "*come*" command, it is possible that Buddy has developed an aversion to that verbal cue. Perhaps, he has learned that the word "*come*" means that it's time to go home and thinks that he is about to get punished, so he doesn't like to cooperate.

Sometimes, dogs also associate this command with a game of chase if the word "*come*" has been used a lot around playtime. If you cannot get your dog to come to you, try using a different command word instead. "Here" is another option that many trainers use instead of "come."

<u>Down!</u>

If you are annoyed by the fact that your ball of fur has to drool on the lap of your visitors, then this command will surely put a stop to it. But that is not the only reason why "*Down*" can be of great importance.

Imagine this scenario: You are walking with your dog off leash when all of a sudden you see him trying to catch the cat he's just spotted across the street. You see a car coming his way, and concerned for his well-being, you shout "*Down*." Your dog drops on the sidewalk and you have just enough time to grab Buddy's collar and attach his leash to it. The upside of "*Down*" in these situations is that, unlike "*Sit*," you are given more time to catch your furry friend as it takes a bit more effort to raise from a "*Down*" position.

Whether you are concerned about his safety, want to stop him from annoying your guests, or you simply want him lying quietly in a café so that you can have your morning coffee in peace, here is how you can teach Buddy the "*Down*" command quickly.

The best (and fastest) strategy is to lure your dog into the "*down*" position instead of waiting for him to lie down on his own. But, in order to do so, you will have to command him to *sit* first. That means that in order for Buddy to master "*down*," he should already have a great understanding of the "*sit*" command. Make sure to start this training only after your dog can learn how to sit on cue.

1. With some treats in your hand, give your dog the "*sit*" command. When he sits down, gently pat him to

acknowledge the good behavior, but do not click or mark the behavior as you usually do. Do not give him the treat just yet. This is important as marking the behavior will give Buddy the signal that he is done performing the desired action, and you may end up losing his attention.

2. Let Buddy see the treat and put it near his nose. Gently lower it to the ground. When you notice Buddy's elbows are about to touch the ground, and he is preparing to lie down, give the **"Down"** command.

3. Once he is fully to the ground, mark the behavior, and give him the treat immediately.

4. Repeat this about a dozen times before using the verbal cue to elicit the behavior. Once Buddy learns what

"Down" means, you are ready to ask for it. Simply say "Down" and wait for the response. If Buddy lies down immediately, then he has already understood the meaning of the exercise. Mark his behavior and lavish him with rewards. If he doesn't do anything, use your empty hand to lure him to the "*down*" position. If that doesn't help either, then you are probably moving too fast. Go back and repeat the steps 1-3 until your dog really catches on.

What If Buddy Stands Up?

It is not uncommon for some dogs to stand up instead of lying down when the treat is lowered to the ground. If that happens, pay attention to how you are lowering the treat. If you are not moving your hand straight down and the treat sort of goes away from his head, your dog will probably get up to follow it. If that is not the issue, however, then you should probably *shape* the command.

Just when your dog starts moving his head to follow the treat, mark the good behavior by using the clicker or making the usual sign. That way, Buddy will understand better that moving toward the floor is what earns the treat.

What If Buddy is Stubborn and Won't Get Down?

If shaping doesn't help Buddy get down either, then you are perhaps dealing with a very stubborn dog. Training a dog that just won't do as you say can be frustrating, but equally successful. All you need is to add a dash of creativity in order to spark Buddy's enthusiasm and motivate him to participate. Here is a creative way to get your Bud down:

1. Sit on the floor next to Buddy, but keep one of your knees high, allowing enough space for him to crawl under it.

2. Lure Buddy to your knee by putting a tasty treat under it. He will have to get down to take it. As soon as you see his elbows touching the ground, say **"Down."**

3. When he lies down completely, mark the behavior immediately, and give him the treat.

If this doesn't help either, then perhaps it is best to give it some time and train Buddy by capturing his behavior. Wait for him to lie down on his own. The moment you notice that he is about to lower his elbows to the ground, say "Down." Then mark, and reward. Repeat this for as long as it takes for him to catch on what the verbal cue means.

Week 2 Training

Now that you have spent a whole week teaching Buddy how to sit, lie down, and come to you, it is time to add a few more words to his dictionary. It is okay if your dog still hasn't learned some of the last week's commands. You can proceed with the training program even if Buddy doesn't quite get how to lie down on cue yet. Just make sure to continue practicing the command he hasn't mastered yet during the second week as well.

Stand!

Okay, you probably will not use the "*stand*" command as often as "*down*" or "*sit*." However, teaching your dog to stand can be of great importance, especially for wiping muddy paws, grooming, vet checks, or simply preventing him from sitting in a muddy puddle.

The best thing about "*Stand*" is that it's perhaps one of the easiest commands to teach, and dogs catch on this concept pretty quickly.

Here is how you can get your Bud to hold a standing position:

1. Instruct your dog to sit in front of you. You should be about one foot away from Buddy.

2. Hold a treat in your hand and lift it in front of his nose, about a few inches away. Then, gently start pulling it upwards. Chances are your dog will stand up to follow it.

3. The moment you notice he is about to stand up, say **"Stand."**

4. Once he is up, click or mark the behavior immediately and give him the treat. If you want your Bud to stand

longer, you can let him nibble on the doggy treat while holding the position.

Practice this about a dozen times or so, until your dog learns what "*stand*" means. Then, you can lure your dog to a standing position while you slowly back away from him. As soon as he is up, say **"Stand"** as you move. If he remains in that position, mark the behavior immediately, and reward him. If not, repeat the steps 1-4 for another dozen times until he really catches on.

The goal here is to fade your movements gradually, until Buddy is able to "*stand*" when he hears the command, without being lured with a treat.

What If Buddy Doesn't Stand Up?

If your dog isn't interested in getting up to follow the treat and just sits there lazily, hoping that you will give it to him, then he is probably not motivated enough. Get creative to entice excitement. Start acting silly, squeak his favorite toy, make funny noises, try jumping up and down… Do whatever it is you think will excite Buddy to stand up. When he is finally in a standing position, mark and reward, to motivate him to repeat the behavior again.

Wait a Second

Saying "Wait" should be just as pressing the *pause* button. It should be a command that will tell your dog to pause for a second and not follow you. It can also serve as a reminder for Buddy that he should defer to you. So, you are not only teaching general behavior here, but you are also instilling good manners.

The most common use of "*wait*" is when the dog owner is about to go out the door and does not want his dog all wired up, thinking he is about to step out into the wonderland too. Because that's what dogs do; they get so excited when they see your hand on the doorknob, that calming them afterward becomes a real headache.

You would think that teaching your overly active dog to "*Wait*" is nearly impossible, but the truth is that this command is one of the easiest to teach. Why? Because you have the best opportunity to train him. How? Since Buddy probably goes in and out of the house a couple of times a day, he can quickly learn that when he "*waits*" for you to open the door first, he gets rewarded by going outside.

1. Go to your front door and instruct your dog to come. Do not take or show the leash to him.

2. Once your dog has joined you in the entryway, wait for him to sit down. You can also instruct him to do so, but the point here is to get him to offer the behavior himself, without being asked.

3. When he finally sits down, say **"Wait"** and make a hand signal to enforce the behavior by putting your hand in front of his nose, with the palm facing him.

4. Now, slowly reach for the doorknob with your hand, and before touching it, mark the behavior either with a clicker, a sound, or simply saying "Good Boy," and give Buddy a yummy treat. If your dog moves before you get the chance to mark the behavior, use a negative word such as **"Oops,"** show him the treat, but do not give it to him. Your dog should learn that he gets rewarded only for good behavior. Wait for him to sit down on his own and repeat the same step until his behavior deserves the treat.

5. Repeat steps 1-3. This time, instead of only reaching for the doorknob, open it

just a crack. Mark the behavior immediately and give Buddy a treat.

6. Again, repeat the first three steps. Now, open the door wider. If Buddy is still waiting, mark and reward. If not, say the negative word and give him the no-reward mark.

7. Gradually open the door wider, until you can step outside and close the door. Once you manage to do that with Buddy still waiting, open the door immediately, go back inside, mark and reward.

The best reward here would be letting your dog out the door as that is what he has been patiently waiting for the whole time, after all. Repeat this a couple of times during the day. Step outside and invite him through after he has been a good boy. Then, play a game of fetch with him in your backyard, take him for a walk, a ride in the car, or do something that Buddy will truly enjoy as a reward.

Caution: If your front door leads directly to the street, practice this method with a safe door. If you have a backyard, your back door can be perfect for this training. If not, place his favorite toys in your bedroom or another room in the house, let him see that, and then close the door. Let Buddy wait in front of the door and try this method there. After he has patiently waited for you to open the door completely and step into the room, invite him in and reward him with a fun game.

What If Buddy Isn't Interested in What's on the Other Side of the Door?

If you cannot get your dog to sit and give you a minute of his attention, or even worse, if he just wanders off and isn't at all interested in what you are trying to reward him with, then perhaps you have lost the battle with the environment. See if you can lower the distractions so you can ensure that Buddy will put his focus on you, try luring him with tastier treats, better toys, etc. or at the end, just leash him. Obviously, you're not supposed to tug on the collar to force him to participate, but a gentle restraint can be quite beneficial in keeping his eyes on the prize.

No Pulling, Mister!

So, you've finally managed to get your dog to accept the collar around his neck and the light pressure of the leash, only to discover that you are nowhere near taking Buddy for a calm walk around the block. Getting your Bud to walk calmly on a leash is perhaps the most challenging thing when it comes to dog training.

It is in your dog's nature to be curious. Dogs want to explore the endless varieties of sights and scents, so running around sniffing and chasing things, to them, is what they are supposed to do when out for a walk. Your dog is born to pull. He probably finds you slow, boring, and since pulling on the leash gets him where he wants to go much faster, he sees nothing wrong in dragging you around the park.

However, even though it may be one of their basic instincts, you shouldn't tolerate it. For Buddy, pulling gets him wherever he wants to go. To put it simply, allowing him to navigate you gets him rewarded.

Perform these steps to teach your dog how not to pull on the leash:

1. Attach the leash to Buddy's collar and go to a place where there aren't many distractions, and where you will be able

to walk in a circle or in a straight line. Have some treats in your pocket.

2. Take the leash with your right hand and put the loop over your thumb. Now, make a fist. Keep your left hand placed just under your right hand, holding the leash with both of your hands. Your hands should be placed as if you were holding a baseball bat.

3. Give him a verbal cue such as **"Let's Go"** or **"Let's Walk,"** and start walking.

4. Just before he gets the chance to get to the other end of the leash and start pulling on it, say **"Easy,"** and immediately make an about-turn to the right, in order to start walking in the opposite direction.

TIP: Hold the leash firmly, but keep in mind that if you keep your entire right hand in through the loop, Buddy might surprise you and make you fall. The loop should be kept over your thumb at all times, so if needed, you can straighten your hand and let it slide off.

5. By holding the leash like you would a baseball bat, and turning in the opposite direction, you are providing a slight pressure on Buddy's collar and prompting him to turn in the new direction.

6. As Buddy is catching up to you, mark the behavior immediately and give him a treat for being such a good boy.

What If Buddy is Just Leaning into His Collar?

If your dog is already leaning into the collar, then you are probably late with your command. Go back to the beginning and make sure you are concentrated. You need to pay attention to how you are giving the cue, the way in which you are holding the leash, but also, you need to learn to anticipate when to make the turn. Watch Buddy and make sure he is focused as well. Be sure to give him the "*Easy*" command first, as this is the cue that you want him to slow down and not to pull. To keep him enthusiastic about the training, provide variety in the rewards and don't let him become bored.

What If Buddy Is Too Strong?

If your dog is too strong and you cannot restrain him, you need to consider getting a different collar in order to prevent him from dragging you around the block. Many trainers say that front-clip no-pull harnesses are the best choice for this purpose. Unlike regular harnesses, these models that have the front clip prevent the dog from pulling that much, as they are designed to turn the dog toward the walker when they begin pulling on the leash.

What If Buddy Pulls Back on the Leash?

In most cases, untrained dogs go in front of the walkers, pulling on the leash and directing them to go whenever they feel like it. However, in some cases, the dog may be pulling back on the leash. This is a sign of fearfulness, which is not uncommon for abandoned or abused dogs. If you've recently adopted your dog or don't know his history, do not rule out that possibility. If this is the case, do not force your dog to learn the no-pull method too quickly as that can only backfire. Instead, work on building up their confidence and strengthening your relationship.

1. Stand near your dog with treats in your hand and wait for him to come to you

voluntarily. Mark the behavior and give him a giant reward. Do this about a dozen times or so.

2. Next, when Buddy comes to you, take out a treat, let him sniff it, but do not give it to him just yet. With the treat in your hand, slowly start walking. Make a couple of steps and then mark the behavior and give Buddy the treat. Repeat this a dozen times.

3. Once you notice Buddy becoming less scared of walking next to you, repeat step 2, only this time, hold the leash like a baseball bat. If Buddy starts to pull back on it, work on step 2 some more. If not, keep walking, marking, and rewarding as you go.

If your dog is fearful, he will probably not pull on the leash. However, he may try to make multiple stops. When that happens, apply gentle pressure on the leash to remind Buddy that you should keep going. Once he takes a step forward, mark, and reward.

The Touch

Touch is the same as targeting. It is basically teaching Buddy to touch a target with his nose, on your command, whether it is the door, some object, or your hand. This is more of a game than it is a behavior, but once you start teaching it to your dog, you will see how much fun it is for him. It is almost like pushing a button; you touch something with your nose, you get a yummy treat. What's not to like?

But, besides being a great way to show off your training skills, the *"touch"* command can also be quite helpful if you are dealing with a stubborn dog who doesn't always listen to you when you tell him to *come*. "*Touch*" is way more enjoyable, and even when the dog doesn't feel like coming to you when you tell him to, giving him the "*touch*" command will most likely change his mind.

"*Touch*" is perfect for the second week of training when you are beginning to teach more challenging behavior. The training will feel like a game and will keep overwhelm at bay.

For "*touch*," you can use pretty much any object. However, I strongly recommend starting with your hand as the target. Your Buddy loves sniffing your hands so it will be much faster and easier to teach him this behavior if you use your hand.

1. Have yummy treats (and the clicker, if you are using one) in one hand. Make sure that the other hand is empty as that will be the target.

2. Stand in front of your dog and gently place your hand near his nose. Your fingers should be pointed down. Wait

for him to sniff it. Once he touches your hand with his nose, mark the behavior, and give him a treat. Repeat this a couple of times in order for Buddy to understand that touching your hand is what gets him rewarded.

3. Repeat the first two steps, only this time, as Buddy prepares to touch your palm with his nose, you say **"Touch."** Then, mark and reward. Practice this a couple of times.

4. Once Buddy gets familiar with the "*touch*" command, you can start moving the target. Back away from your dog and see if he will follow it. Place it in different angles at nose level. Once he becomes more confident, you can try placing the target on the floor, a bit higher, etc.

When Buddy masters the "*touch*" behavior with your hand, you can then try it with different objects.

What If Buddy Doesn't Touch Your Hand?

If Buddy is confused and is not interested at all in touching your palm with his nose, it is perhaps because your other hand distracts him. Make sure to keep your hand with the treats (and clicker) behind your back so that Buddy can only see your empty hand.

If that is not the issue, then try to entice him to sniff and touch your hand. Rub a treat on your target hand before offering it to him. If this does the trick, repeat it for as long as it takes for Buddy to master "*touch*." However, make sure to gradually fade out the scent in order to avoid Bud from becoming dependent on the yummy aroma.

Week 3 Training

During the third week, you will most likely notice significant progress in the way in which Buddy responds to the training sessions. If you have been following this book's instructions right, then he already knows the basic commands and gets pretty enthusiastic to get the behavior right in the hope of getting a yummy reward.

This is the time when you should introduce more advanced techniques and take his behavior to a whole new level. Of course, you should also continue practicing the commands that he is already familiar with, but make sure to gradually increase the environmental distractions (having the cat in the same room, doing it in the backyard with your toddler running around, etc.) so that you can prepare him for uncertainties in the real world and teach him how to respond to your commands the right way during these situations.

Walk Nicely by My Side

When it comes to dog walking, most dog owners confuse heeling with being able to walk on a loose leash. And while the latter is a skill that your dog absolutely has to have mastered in order for you to take him out for a nice walk, there are times when you will simply need him to "*heel.*"

Heeling means walking on your left side, on your command. It is very different than loose leash walking when Buddy is on his own, sniffing around and chasing pigeons. When he is at your heel, your dog focuses on you every step of the way. He walks nicely by your side, whether you make a left turn, slow down, or decide to run. Heeling is a behavior that will be greatly appreciated when walking on a crowded and busy sidewalk or at times when you will need to have absolute control. If you are planning to sign up Buddy for obedience competition, keep in mind that he must master the "*heel*" command first.

But, before you jump straight to teaching your Buddy how to walk nicely by your side, you should first introduce sitting at heel, in order for your dog to get the handle of this command and become familiar with it. Here is how you can do it:

1. Place some treats in your pocket. Attach Buddy's leash to his collar and instruct him to sit down. Make sure that he is sitting on your left side, and that you are both facing in the same direction. Put the leash over your shoulder. It is best to have Buddy sitting down on your left side and his leash placed over your right shoulder

2. With your right foot, take one step forward. Then, take a step with your left foot but make sure to put the left foot past your right. Drop your right knee down and place your hand on Buddy's chest. Gently fold him to readjust his position from sitting to sitting at heel, saying **"Heel"** in a firm but positive tone, at the same time.

3. Immediately mark the behavior and give him a treat.

4. Keep in mind that Buddy knows how to sit, you just need to show him where you want him to do it. Repeat for as long as it takes for Buddy to understand what "*heel*" means. Just make sure not to push on his rear end, and each time you're saying "*heel*," gradually decrease the physical assistance, giving Buddy

the chance to catch on and eventually do this on his own.

Now that Buddy knows where he is supposed to go when he hears the word "*heel,*" it is time for you to teach him to actually walk at heel. To do so, perform these steps:

1. Attach Buddy's leash to his collar. Instruct him to sit at heel, again, you should both be facing the same direction. Place the leash over your right shoulder, but make sure to allow some slack (about 4 inches or so) to ensure that there will be no tension on his collar when you start walking.

2. With your hands close to your body and at waist height, make a funnel around the leash. The point of this is so you can avoid touching the leash when there is no need for it.

3. Give the **"Heel"** command in a firm but positive tone and start walking in a brisk way. The pace here is really important as your goal is to prompt Buddy to take a step forward. If you start slowly, Buddy will not get the message. He will most likely just sit at heel and wait for his reward there. But if you start at a fast pace, as if you are running late, his first instinct will be to follow your step. You can either walk in a straight line or a large circle in a clockwise motion.

4. The goal of this exercise is to get Buddy to walk nicely by your left side. However, once he starts walking, you will notice that he is not that interested in walking at heel. When he leaves your side, lock your hands around the leash to apply some tension and return him back to the "*heel*" position. Anytime Buddy tries to get ahead of you, bring him back to

your side. His shoulder should be in line with your left hip.

5. Make a couple of steps, then stop, mark the behavior, and lavish him with verbal praises and treats.

6. Repeat this a dozen times, each time adding a couple more steps. It will take a few tries before Buddy can understand what you are trying to achieve. Just make sure to put energy into your walking in order to keep his focus on you. Make it your initial goal to make 10 steps without touching the leash. Once you manage to achieve that, it won't be long before Buddy masters this command completely.

What If Buddy is Very Stubborn?

If your dog is fighting you and you cannot get him to make a couple of steps without him trying to take the lead, then perhaps you should try luring him with treats:

1. Instruct him to "*sit*" on your left side. Attach the leash and place it over your right shoulder, again, allowing about 4 inches of slack. Place some treats in your left hand.

2. Keep your right hand at waist height, and make a tunnel around the leash. Hold the treat hand near Buddy's nose.

3. Give him the "**Heel**" command and start walking at a brisk pace. Keep your hand with the treat in front of Buddy to lure him to take a step forward.

4. Make a couple of steps, then stop, mark the behavior, and give Buddy the treat.

5. Repeat this 5-6 times, each time increasing the distance. Once Buddy becomes comfortable with the

maneuver, try this exercise without the treat.

Changing Direction

Congratulations! Your dog can now walk in a straight line (or a circle) calmly by your left side. But are you two ready to make it through a crowded place just yet? Before you fool yourself into thinking you are ready to handle traffic, you need to make sure that Buddy can stay at heel even when making a turn.

Right Turn

In order for your dog to continue walking at heel when you are making a right turn, your ball of fur will need to increase his pace. If you try this now, you will probably end up turning right while Buddy will continue walking in the other direction. At this stage, when your dog is still new to training and is not able to give you a hundred percent, you need to trick him into making a turn as well.

Instruct Buddy to walk at heel. Before you make a right turn, say his name in an upbeat tone. When he looks up at you, make the turn, and continue walking. Hearing his name will cause Buddy to look at you, which will help him notice that you are changing the direction. That way, he can stay with you even when making a right turn.

About-Turn

An about-turn, technically, is making a right turn twice. Which means that you will need to say Buddy's name twice, in order to keep his attention and make sure that he continues walking at heel.

If he has trouble following you, you can lure him into making a turn with a treat. But, since most dogs become overly stimulated by this method, make sure not to use the treat lure unless you absolutely have to.

Left Turn

If you try to make a left turn now, you will probably bump into Buddy. For this turn, Buddy does not need to look at you but to slow down his pace so you can both make a left turn, safely.

But for him to slow down, you have to slow down, first. So, instruct the *"heel,"* start walking, and then slow down the pace. Draw back on his leash using your left hand, and then slowly make the left turn. After doing so, return your hand back to its initial position (the funnel around the leash), and resume your faster pace.

Down from a Distance

This is, perhaps, one of the most important commands that you can teach your dog. Once you can command him to drop down on a dime, even from across the street, then you've achieved an incredible control of Buddy's activity.

Okay, but doesn't "*come*" do the same thing? Sure, if you see that your ball of fur is chasing a squirrel and is about to cross a busy street to get it, you can use the "*come*" command to get him to stop. However, when you say "*come*," you are actually asking Buddy to stop, turn around, come back to you and forget all about the squirrel. That's simply a lot to ask. And since your dog is probably super determined to get that squirrel, at such challenging times, the "*come*" command may not even work.

The "*down,*" command, on the other hand, is a lot different. First of all, when you shout "*Down*" from a distance, all you're asking Buddy to do is to simply drop down to the ground. He doesn't even have to move his eyes away from the squirrel. After a couple of seconds, when you get to Buddy, his arousal level will have already decreased, so it will be much easier for him to shift his attention to you.

Here is how you can train Buddy to drop down from a distance:

1. Attach the leash to his collar and stand in front of him, facing him. Hold the leash with one hand and then instruct Buddy to "*sit.*"

2. Now, gently take a step back, and give him the **"Down"** command. Since Buddy has been practicing "*Down*" from Week 1, chances are he is already pretty good at this command by now.

3. When he lays down, immediately mark the behavior and give him a treat.

4. It is super <u>important</u> to add some variety to this training. If you give Buddy the "*down*" command every time you take a step or two backward, he will soon associate the command with your steps, and will most likely begin offering the behavior every time he notices you are about to step away, as he will have learned that making a step backward means "*down*" and reward. To avoid that, keep the exercise unpredictable. Sometimes, take a step backward, mark the behavior, and then return to Buddy to give him the reward. Or ask Buddy to "*sit*" when you step away.

5. Once Buddy begins offering the "*down*" position easily, start increasing the distance. Instead of making one step, take two steps backward. Then take three, four... Gradually increase the distance until Buddy will have no

problem laying down even if you give him the command from across the room.

When you manage that, see how you will do without the leash and without instructing Buddy to "*sit*" first. Practice for as long as it takes for your dog to become comfortable laying down when you tell him to, even if he is on his own time, digging in the backyard or sniffing around in the park off-leash.

What If Buddy Doesn't Want to Lie Down?

Keep in mind that your dog already knows the "*down*" command. He has learned that "*down*" is performed from a sitting position when you are next to him. He is probably just confused because you have decided to change the rules of the "*down*" he is familiar with. Make sure that you are not more than one step away from him, and do not increase the distance before he becomes more comfortable with the new game. Step away, ask for the "*down*" and wait a couple of seconds. If Buddy won't do it even when you are just a step away, then lure him with a treat by lowering it to the ground. Click and reward. Repeat this until your dog can do this without the lure. Then try by taking two steps, then three, and so on.

Stay Longer

Many new owners think that "*stay*" and "*wait*" are the same, so they often use both commands to elicit the same behavior. But that is a huge mistake to make. "*Stay*" is a very different command than the "*wait*" exercise that we covered in the second week. While "*wait*" means "pause," "*stay*" means "hold that position until I tell you otherwise."

You can see how different they are, as well as how confusing using them interchangeably can be for Buddy. For instance, if you are about to leave your house and go to work, you tell your Buddy to "*wait*" in order for him to give you some space to go outside and close the door. You don't tell him to "*stay,*" which technically means "do not move from that spot until I get back from work," as that's impossible.

<u>The Three D's</u>

According to most trainers, the *stay* command has three main elements:

#1: **D**uration – how long your dog *stays*

#2: **D**istractions – how capable the dog is to *stay* when distractions are present

#3: **D**istance – how far you will move away from your dog when you ask him to *stay*

These three elements are incredibly important for the training process of this command, and, therefore, it is critical for you to follow the order, meaning that you should work on the duration first, then introduce distractions, and finally, instruct the command from a distance.

Here is how you can teach your Bud to "*stay*" in a certain position:

1. Instruct Buddy to "*sit.*" Praise him verbally and then hold up a treat. Wait for a second, then mark the behavior and give him the reward. Make sure to feed Buddy calmly to prevent him from jumping up.

2. Use a release word to encourage your Buddy to get up. Most people choose "Okay" for the release word, but if you are using okay in conversation often, you might choose another one to avoid confusing your dog. *Release, Get Up, Free, Break, At Ease, Done,* etc. are all good examples for a release word. When Buddy gets up, you can give him another treat to reward him for being a good boy, but do not mark the behavior. You are teaching "*stay*" after all, so you

should put the emphasis on that command.

3. Repeat the process again, only this time, say **"Stay"** when you show him the treat. Hold the treat up for 2 seconds and make sure to place it either under Buddy's nose or far enough so he will not be able to nibble on it.

4. Mark the behavior and give him the treat. Use the release word to encourage him to get up.

5. Repeat, but this time, try to hold the treat for 3 seconds. Working on the *duration* is very important, so repeat this for as long as it takes for Buddy to be able to maintain that position for ten seconds. Make sure to use the verbal cue all the way through, to remind him that he should "*stay*."

6. Once Buddy is able to "*stay*" for longer than 10 seconds, you can then introduce small distractions. Instruct him to "*stay*" and then take a hop. Immediately mark the behavior, give him the treat, and release. Repeat the "*stay*" again, hop on one foot, wait for a second, then hop on the other foot. Mark, reward, release. Gradually build up the distractions until your Buddy is able to "*stay*" even when you are hopping up and down, clapping your hands, spinning in a circle, etc. Remember to introduce distractions gradually. You want Buddy to succeed in mastering the "*stay*."

7. When your dog is able to remain in the same position for about 20-30 seconds with distractions, you can then start working on the third D – the distance. However, you cannot instruct him to

"*stay*" from a distance when there are distractions present. Remove the distractions, take a step away from your dog, and instruct Buddy to "*stay.*" Mark, reward, release. The second time, take two steps away. Then three, four, five... Gradually increase the distance, but <u>always return to Buddy to reward him.</u> Do not call your dog to come to you from a distance, as that may motivate him to break the "*stay*" in order to come to you and get the reward.

8. When your dog can "*stay*" even when you are not near him, you can gradually start combining the three D's.

The technique above is for teaching Buddy to "*stay*" from a sitting position. You can also use the same method to teach him to remain in a "*down*" position. Simply, instead of instructing him to "*sit,*" tell Buddy to lie "*down*" before teaching him the "*stay.*"

What if Buddy Gets Up Before You Release Him?

If your dog gets up before you give him the release word, then you should include a negative punishment to motivate him to remain in that position in order to get the reward. Just put your hand with the treat behind your back, and say "*Oops,*" to let Buddy know that he has done something wrong. Then, wait a couple of seconds and repeat again. Instruct him to "*sit,*" then hold up the treat where he can see it. He needs to understand that getting up without hearing the release word makes the treat go away. If he gets up again, do it all over. Repeat this for as long as it takes for Buddy to get the message.

Relax!

How many times have you forced yourself to go out or fake a smile and ended up having a good time and genuinely smiling? We often need to be reminded to hit the pause button and just relax. Your Bud has had a pretty intense week. You have been teaching him three challenging commands that soak up a lot of his energy. Even if his constant jumping up and down tells you otherwise, your dog probably craves rest. Sometimes, you should remind him to take a rest after a long day to nurture his mental being and preserve his strength for the following training.

Teaching Buddy to "*relax,*" basically means telling him to go lie down on his side. Besides the fact that this command will help him recharge his batteries, it is also needed for some of the most popular games you can play with your dog.

1. Instruct Buddy to lie down. Once he does that, give him a treat, but do not mark the behavior. Remember, you should put the emphasis on "*relax,*" not "*down.*"

2. Now, take a look at his "*down*" position. In order for you to teach him the "*relax,*" Buddy needs to be lying on his hip, with his hind legs to the side. If that is the case, you can skip this step.

3. If Buddy is not in that position and is in a perfect square, you need to rock him onto his hip. To do so, place a treat in front of Buddy's nose, then move it toward the place between his hip and shoulder, making a semicircle. Buddy will most likely follow the yummy treat with his nose and rock onto his hip on his own. Mark the behavior and give him the treat.

4. Once your dog is on his side, move the treat over the point of his spine, until Buddy begins to roll onto his side. Once he starts doing that and ends up in a "C" curl, move the reward toward his head to the floor, in front of his nose. Now, this is the moment where your dog is supposed to put his head to the floor in order to get the treat. As soon as he does that, say **"Relax,"** then mark the behavior and give Buddy the reward.

5. Repeat luring Buddy into this position, until he becomes really familiar with it and starts offering it easily. Then, you can phase out the lure, and start giving the verbal cue to elicit the behavior.

What If Buddy Is Tense and Won't Relax?

If you are dealing with a tense dog who refuses to turn his head all the way, then you need to shape the behavior. Watch your dog's behavior and notice when he makes the jump up. Most tense dogs just move their heads a few inches and then jump up, refusing to rock onto the hip. If that is the case, you need to increase the turn gradually, inch by inch. Note after how many inches your dog jumps up. If he turns his head 4 inches, then mark his behavior after the third inch and give him a reward. Next time, do it after 4 inches, and so on until he is encouraged to turn all the way.

Week 4 Training

After three weeks of training, your dog is now not only ready to take a nice walk and come to you when called, but he is also able to remain in a certain position until you tell him otherwise, as well as to drop down even when instructed from a distance. That surely makes life with a canine a lot easier and more entertaining. However, you still have a long way to go before you can actually brag to your friends about having a well-mannered ball of fur.

Before you jump to teaching Buddy fun games to show off your training skills, you first need to make sure that he masters a few more important commands:

Take It!

Having a dog that has mastered the skill to retrieve is one of the most important indicators that you have succeeded in training. The "*take it*" command is the starting point for mastering retrieve, and it is also the easiest thing to teach. Since your dog does nothing but *take* things pretty much most of the time, you will have tons of opportunities to capture the desired behavior on a daily basis. But since taking things is something Buddy enjoys, jumping straight to the verbal cue shouldn't be a problem:

1. Start with something that you know Buddy will take, like his favorite doggy treats. Place one in your hand, stand next to Buddy, show him the treat, and say **"Take It."**

2. As he closes his jaw to get the treat, mark the behavior so that he understands that that's the desired behavior.

3. Repeat the same process, but make it a bit more challenging by placing the treat someplace where Buddy shouldn't be able to get it as easily. For instance, place the treat behind you or even better, move your hand away as you offer him the treat so that he will have to follow it. Say **"Take It,"** let him have the treat and mark the behavior.

4. Then, try it with his favorite toy. Make a squeaky sound to get his attention and

get him excited. Tease him with the toy a bit before offering it to him. As his mouth closes on it, mark the behavior and give him a reward to encourage him to repeat it. Now, he will probably drop the toy to get his reward, but that's okay. The point is to "*take*" the object when you are offering it, not to hold it.

5. Once he is familiar with taking things from your hand, let him practice this on the floor. Toss his toy in front of you, and as you do it, say "**Take It.**" Once he picks it up, mark the behavior, and give him the reward. If your Buddy doesn't want to pick objects off the floor, try to gradually decrease your hand to the floor when you are practicing this command, to get him used to taking things from that height.

6. Gradually increase the distance by tossing the toy further away. It won't be long before you can spend an hour playing fetch in your backyard.

What If Buddy Refuses to Take Things?

No dog will refuse to take yummy treats from your hand (unless he is dealing with some medical issues), that's a fact. But what if your dog takes his favorite toy and treats with ease but is not interested in taking other objects that you are offering him?

If your dog doesn't want to take other things, try to shape the behavior:

1. Instruct Buddy to "*take"* an object. If he refuses, place the object on the floor, or on a chair, and step away. Let him explore it first.

2. Every time he looks at the object, mark the behavior and give him a treat. Once

he realizes that the object gives him the reward, he will be encouraged to go near it, and maybe even *"touch"* it with his nose. When he does that, mark and reward. Make sure to stop rewarding Buddy for looking at the object when he starts touching it with his nose.

3. As the touches become more frequent, he will eventually open his mouth to make contact. When that happens, lavish him with treats, give him his favorite toy, play a game, etc. The point is to celebrate the performed behavior to let Buddy know how positive *"taking"* that object is. Again, once he *"takes it,"* stop rewarding him for touching it so that he can get the message.

4. Perform this with other objects as well. Chances are, teaching *"take it"* to Buddy

now is a lot easier than it was in the beginning.

<u>Give!</u>

As beneficial teaching "*take it*" can be, trust me, having your dog master "*give*" will have an even greater significance. Since Buddy loves playing the "*take it*" game so much, he will be running around with a valuable and forbidden object in his mouth sooner rather than later. When that happens, begging and pleading with your dog will not do the trick. Bribing him with a piece of sausage may also be risky as he may drop down the object and end up causing damage. Besides, what if you don't have any yummy bribes with you?

For these situations, the "*give*" command is a true lifesaver. "*Giving*" you objects on cue can teach Buddy that not everything you own should be used to play a round of chase-me.

1. Fill your pockets with doggy treats. Take Buddy's favorite toy in one hand. Squeak or shake it to get his attention. Once he gets excited, offer the toy to him or simply drop it on the floor so he can catch it.

2. When he has it in his mouth, grab a treat and show it to him, while saying **"Give."**

3. When Buddy opens his mouth to take the treat, he'll drop the toy on the floor. Mark the behavior. With your other hand, gently take the toy. Let Buddy nibble on the treat, but do not give him the whole thing until you have the toy in your other hand.

4. Once you are holding the toy, show it to Buddy and give him the whole treat.

5. Practice this for as long as it takes for your dog to start *"giving"* you his toys willingly. When that's achieved, you should be able to retrieve a forbidden object just as easily.

What If Buddy Loves Playing with the Toy but Refuses to Give a Forbidden Object?

If your dog has learned the *"give"* command with his toy but when the time comes to really *"give"* a forbidden object, he refuses, it probably is because he already knows that *"giving"* you the object means game over. Do not just take things from him; make sure to spend some time playing the *"give"* game as well. It doesn't matter if Buddy knows what *"give"* means. Continue playing the *"give"* game with his toy (when Buddy actually gets the toy at the end), in order to keep him enthusiastic about the word *"give."*

Also, do not forget to lavish him with treats whenever he "*gives"* you a forbidden object.

Caution: *Do NOT practice this command if your dog growls, tenses, or tries to bite when approaching her to get the object. If Buddy shows any signs of aggression, immediately seek help from a qualified trainer or behavior professional.*

Leave It!

Once you start going on longer walks, you will notice that the thing that Buddy loves the most is chewing on stuff he finds in the park. And most of these times, those things will be truly disgusting. That's when telling him to leave stuff alone comes in handy. Being able to tell Buddy to "*leave"* the sharp bone piece he spotted in the gutter can be truly beneficial. Not to mention how useful this command can be when setting up the dinner table or when

Buddy gets tempted to steal the pizza slice that your toddler has been nibbling on for hours.

Here is how you can teach a basic, "*leave it*" command:

1. Hold a treat that is not squishable (freeze-dried meat works best) in front of Buddy. Have a few more treats in your other hand, and hold them behind your back.

2. Make sure you have Buddy's attention, and then place the treat under your foot's ball." At the same time, firmly say **"Leave It."** Buddy can sniff and nibble on the treat, but do not let him have it. You should think about wearing shoes that cannot be damaged.

3. The point here is to wait for Buddy to give up and stop licking the treat. When

that happens, mark the behavior immediately, and give him the treat.

4. Gradually start increasing the delay between the time Buddy "*leaves*" the treat and the time you mark the behavior so that he can stay away from the yummy piece of liver for longer periods.

5. Repeat this for as long as it takes for Buddy to start "*leaving*" the treat alone when he hears the verbal cue "*Leave It.*" When he can manage to resist touching the treat for a few seconds, practice a bit more tempting exercise. This time, try to cover only half of the treat with your foot, leaving half uncovered and free to be nibbled on. If Buddy dives to take the uncovered liver, cover it with your foot quickly, and say **"Oops."** Your dog needs to understand that reaching for

the treat makes the reward go away. Then mark and reward him. Repeat this for as long as it takes for him to be able to resist the temptation and *leave* uncovered treats alone for a few seconds.

What If Buddy Cannot Stop Licking?

You need to be patient. Eventually, Buddy will realize that he cannot reach the treat, and he will just give up. If you think that the licking is taking longer than it's supposed to, then perhaps Buddy can reach the treat from under your foot. See if you can tip the foot to keep him away from the prize. Keep in mind that if he can touch the treat, he is being reinforced and, therefore, will never learn how to "*leave it*" properly.

Leave It When Dropped

Imagine this scenario: You are making a ham sandwich when all of a sudden, your hand slips and the entire container with leftover ham slices drops on the floor. Buddy, who has been sitting beside you the whole time hoping that you will reward him with a slice, doesn't think twice about diving into that container. Will *"Leave It"* work when such a tempting situation occurs? In order to prepare Buddy (and yourself) for these temptations, a good amount of practice is required first. Make sure to exercise the *"Leave It"* game when tasty treats are dropped in order to train Buddy to leave stuff alone even when it's super hard to resist.

1. Instruct Buddy to sit in front of you. With a firm but positive tone, say **"Leave It"** and immediately drop a yummy treat so that it falls on the side and slightly behind you. This is important as you will need to get in front of the treat if Buddy's first instinct is to grab it.

2. Wait for Buddy to look away once he realizes that he cannot reach the sausage piece. When that happens, mark the behavior and let him have the treat.

3. Repeat this and gradually start placing the treat in places where you cannot guard it from him, until Buddy is ready to "*leave it*" on cue, regardless of where you've dropped it.

4. But since in temptation alley the food will be dropped first, you need to turn the exercise around and try to drop the treat first, and then tell Buddy to "*leave it.*" Again, if necessary, block the treat to prevent Buddy from reaching it. Practice for as long as it takes for Buddy to be able to resist the urge to grab the treat.

What If Buddy Cannot Resist the Temptation When Out for a Walk?

If your dog has already mastered the "*Leave It*" command at home and looks the other way when you tell him not to take the dropped lasagna from the floor, but struggles to pay attention to your commands when someone drops a piece of hot dog in the park, then perhaps you should work on the exercise a bit more:

1. Ask a family member or a friend to help you out. Put Buddy on a leash, allowing a slack of a couple of inches. Give your friend some doggy food that Buddy doesn't particularly love, and position them so that they are about 20 feet away from you.

2. Let your accomplice start walking toward you, dropping treats along the way. Grab Buddy's leash and stroll

toward your friend as well. Give Buddy the **"Leave It"** cue and continue walking. Make sure to restrain Buddy so that he cannot reach the treats. Once you are out of the 'danger zone' (the treats' vicinity), mark Buddy's behavior, and give him a tasty treat as a reward.

3. After 2-3 repetitions, let your friend drop tastier treats. Do the same thing and gradually increase the taste of the treats until you have some really irresistible pieces of liver dropped on the floor. The goal is to have Buddy look the other way. Until that happens, keep restraining him to prevent him from reaching for the treats. This is really important as reaching the treat means reinforcing the behavior.

4. Once you are at least 80 percent sure that you don't have to put pressure on

the leash and that Buddy will look the other way when you give him the verbal cue, then you can try practicing the same exercise in different locations. Try your backyard, the nearest park, an uncrowded sidewalk, etc. Finally, try this exercise without the leash. If Buddy offers the *"Leave It"* behavior willingly, he is ready for the endless temptations of the outer world.

Go to Your Place

No matter how much you love spending your afternoons with your furry friend, there will be times when you will simply need to hit a pause and break from Buddy's company. Sometimes, your dog will have the same need, as well. Every dog needs to have its own place in the home. Someplace where they can go to sleep, be alone, or just relax after a good meal. A place where you can send Buddy to when you want to have a quiet dinner, or when your old aunt comes to visit.

Method 1

The first method is teaching Buddy how to go to his spot by shaping his behavior. Shaping "*go to your place,*" means allowing your dog to fully engage his brain, which can also be beneficial for other exercises as well.

By shaping, you simply set up the environment to let Buddy perform the behavior, then you mark and reward. It's a fun way to teach and learn:

1. Place a mat (or a rug) on the floor. Have your Buddy nearby and fill your pockets with treats.

2. Watch Buddy's behavior closely. You are simply waiting for him to associate with the placed mat. Every time he looks at

the mat, immediately mark the behavior and give him a treat.

3. Once you notice that Buddy is getting closer to the mat, mark immediately and give him the treat, but either throw the treat behind you or place it on the floor near you. The point is for Buddy to get away from the mat and "reset" his movement by returning to you. That way, you can begin the practice from scratch.

4. Eventually, Buddy will catch on and understand that getting closer to the mat gets him rewarded. Once he starts getting closer to the mat easily, try to get him to sit. To tell your dog that you want him to go to his place, you need a verbal cue. *Mat, Place, Spot, Settle,* are all good examples.

5. The point here is to wait for Buddy to sit or lie down on the mat on his own. The instant that happens, say **"Place"** or whatever cue you want to use, mark, and reward. Repeat for as long as it takes for Buddy to associate that cue word with that mat. You can then place the mat in your kitchen, living room, or wherever you want Buddy to settle, and ask your dog to go to his spot and be alone for a while.

Keep in mind that this method takes patience, but it is also more beneficial as this way you allow your dog to engage his mind and learn how to solve problems on his own. If this is too overwhelming for you, or if you don't have the time for shaping, try the luring method below.

Method 2

1. Place the mat on the floor. Call Buddy in the same room and make sure you are

both standing about two feet from the mat.

2. Hold a yummy treat in your hand. Show the hand to Buddy and gently lure him to the mat with the treat hand. Say "**Place**" or your preferred verbal cue, at the same time.

3. Once Buddy is standing on the mat, instruct him to "*Sit.*" Mark the behavior and reward him with the treat.

4. Repeat this a few times and make sure to point toward the mat with your treat hand while saying the verbal cue.

5. After a few repetitions, instead of instructing Buddy to sit, use the "*down*" command. Make sure to reward Buddy for staying in his place to help him associate the mat as something positive that gets him rewarded.

6. Once Buddy starts to catch on, use the verbal cue and then wait to see what his reaction will be. If he starts walking toward the mat, mark, and reward. While rewarding him for getting closer to the mat, start moving farther away. This is important as, ultimately, the "*Go to your spot*" command should be instructed from a distance.

Tip: Trick Buddy into falling in love with the mat. Make sure to put treats and all sorts of lovely surprises there for him to find, so he can think of 'his spot' as something positive and rewarding, not a place where he will be lonely.

Dealing with Misbehavior

You have managed to successfully house train your dog and teach him all of the commands from above. Congratulations! You can now take long walks even off-leash, without the fear of Buddy's (or other living species') wellbeing. But even though your Buddy knows the meaning of a lot of your English words, he still has a long way to go before becoming the wonderfully well-mannered pet.

Dogs often show a lot of behavioral problems that are not only bad and annoying, but sometimes dangerous, as well. Here are some of the most common ways in which dogs misbehave and how to prevent them from happening:

Excessive Barking

No one likes having a barker around. Besides the fact that your neighbors are definitely not appreciating Buddy's loud barking, keep in mind that this problematic behavior is also illegal in some places. For the sake of everyone in Buddy's vicinity, you need to come up with a way to put a stop to his excessive barking. But in order to do that, you need to first pinpoint why your dog is barking in the first place. Assuming that you have ruled out the possibility that your dog is dealing with a medical issue or is barking because he needs to go potty, here are the different types of barkers and how to shush them:

Request Barking

Request barking is one of the most common problems that dog owners have. It happens when your dog is seeking your attention and barks in hopes of getting the thing he wants from you.

Do not Reinforce. The first step you need to take to stop your dog from attention barking is to simply stop giving him what he wants. Of course, keep in mind that this cannot happen overnight and that you will probably need some time to teach him that request barking gets him no positive results, especially if he is already used to getting what he wants with each bark.

Ignore His Barking. However, simply stopping the reinforcement will probably not do the trick, or it will take a lot of time for him to understand that he is doing it in vain. Meanwhile, try to ignore his request barking. Keep in mind that in Buddy's mind, even telling him to stop is giving him attention. This will lead to no positive results but will most likely only encourage him to continue barking. When Buddy is barking, simply go about your day. Do not give him a shred of attention. In fact, do not even look at him. Just keep yourself distracted and try not to think too much of how annoying his barking sound is.

Reward the Silence. Here is where positive reinforcement comes in handy. Once your dog stops barking, immediately mark the behavior, either with a clicker, by making a sound that you will use for marking or simply by telling Buddy that he has been a good boy. Then, give him a yummy treat. Do this every time Buddy stops his barking. Over time, your dog will learn that becoming silent gives him rewards, which will motivate him to stop barking.

Once he catches on, you need to work on delaying the rewards, otherwise, Buddy will play a bark-and-stop game in order to get treated as often as possible. Do the exercise from above for a couple of days. The third day, when Buddy stops barking, wait a couple of seconds before giving him the treat. Wait for 5 seconds, then 10, and work your way up until Buddy waits for a minute or two in silence before getting the reward.

Tip: Vary the length of time between the moment your dog stops barking, and when you give him the treat. That way, Buddy will not become used to getting rewards and will not come to expect a piece of sausage after a certain amount of time.

Find an Alternative Behavior. I agree that replacing his attention-seeking desires with training lessons or other exercises may be time-consuming and somewhat overwhelming, but there is no doubt that this is the best way to teach your dog if he wants your attention, he has to engage in other activities. That creates an amazing opportunity for you to teach Buddy desirable behavior, whether it is a new command you have been working on or a fun game to pass the time. So, instead of responding to his requests, instruct Buddy to sit and teach him something else while you have his undivided attention.

Alarm Barking

It is nice to have your dog give you a heads-up when there is someone at the door. But if Buddy perceives everyone passing near your house to be an intruder and starts barking loudly for hours, now that is surely a problem.

You can easily recognize alarm barking. With each bark, the dog alarm barking pounces forward or makes a slight lunge.

The "Quiet" Command

Believe it or not, you can actually teach your dog to stop barking excessively on cue. It doesn't matter how territorial Buddy is; if you are consistent about the training routine and patient enough to let your dog succeed, you will soon teach him to stop barking on cue, just like you instruct him to sit down.

1. Once you notice that your dog is alarm barking, grab a treat and show it to him.

This should be enough for him to get distracted and shift his attention to you.

2. Wait until your dog stops barking. The second he stops, firmly say **"Quiet."** Then, immediately mark the behavior and give Buddy the treat.

3. Repeat this every time you notice your dog guarding his territory and barking at perceived intruders. After a dozen repetitions or so, you can start giving him the verbal cue *"quiet"* before he stops barking to elicit the behavior. Of course, that means that you also shouldn't be showing him the treat anymore, but wait for him to earn it. If Buddy complies, mark the behavior and give him the treat. If not, then you probably need to lure him with the treat some more. Eventually, he will learn to do it without the freeze-dried liver.

4. Now that you think your dog can actually stop barking on cue, it is time to apply this command and test his behavior. Have a friend slam the car door upfront or make a noise in front of your house. Wait for Buddy's reaction with a treat in your hand. If Buddy starts barking, say **"Quiet,"** but do not show him the treat. If he stops, mark the behavior and reward him. If not, then you probably need to spend some more time training.

Discouraging Jumping Up

All dogs love jumping up. And to be honest, most of us like that too. Except when the dog is covered in mud or when he is about to knock down your 95-year-old uncle. But it is in their nature to jump. In fact, when we pick them up as puppies and cuddle them near our chest, we actually reinforce the jumping behavior. If that is not as cute as it was when Buddy was a cuddly ball of fur and you want to discourage this behavior, you first have to get everybody on board and make sure that none of you will encourage the behavior by rewarding it with patting and smooches.

Below you will find an on-leash and off-leash exercise that you need to perform with Buddy in order to train him not to jump up on you, as well as a tried-and-true technique to stop Buddy from greeting visitors too enthusiastically.

The On-Leash Exercise

1. Have a friend or a family member help you out with this exercise. Give him a treat and ask him to start approaching you and Buddy. Call Buddy and attach the leash to his collar.

2. Hold Buddy's leash and make sure to stand still. Tell your friend to start approaching you and to hold the treat up against his chest.

3. Do not allow leash slack so Buddy cannot get up. Once he notices that he cannot jump up to your helper to get the treat, he will eventually get frustrated and sit down. The instant he does that, mark the behavior, and let your friend give him the treat.

4. Repeat this process about a dozen times. It usually takes dogs about 5-6 repetitions to figure out that sitting down when being approached is what gets them rewarded. If your dog needs more training to catch on, don't worry. Keep repeating until Buddy starts to sit down willingly.

5. After a dozen repetitions, try again, but this time, offer a few inches of slack. Let your friend approach you with the treat up against his chest. Wait for Buddy's reaction. If his first instinct is to sit down, then he has already learned the point. Mark the behavior and give him the treat immediately. If he jumps up to get the treat, have your friend whisk out the reward and firmly say **"Oops."**

6. Once Buddy sits down again, mark the behavior, and give him the treat.

When you don't have a friend to help you out, you can try this on your own. Simply, attach Buddy's leash to something, allowing a little slack. Stand about 10 feet away from him and wait for Buddy to sit down. Start approaching him. As long as he is sitting down, keep approaching until you get close to him to mark and reward. The instant Buddy jumps up, stop, say **"Oops"** and whisk out the treat. Eventually, he will learn that sitting calmly gets him rewarded.

The Off-Leash Exercise

But what about those times when you walk through the door and Buddy greets you in an overly excited, almost brutal way? There is surely no way to leash restrain him there. When that happens, the best tactic is to simply *ignore* him.

1. Keep a jar with doggy treats in the entryway or have biscuits with you all the time. Walk through the door and see what Buddy's reaction is.

2. If he starts jumping up, simply look away and avoid eye contact. From the corner of your eye, watch Buddy's movements and when he is about to jump up on you, step away from him.

3. Wait for Buddy to get frustrated for not getting his attention and sit down. The instant he does that, mark the behavior with a clicker, a kissing sound, or by telling him that he is a good boy. Then, give him the reward.

4. Keep repeating this every time you walk through the front door until Buddy realizes that sitting down gets him rewarded.

Jumping Up on Guests

The on-leash and off-leash exercises are great for teaching your Buddy to give you some space when you come home from work. But will they work when you have your sister and her toddlers come for a visit? I don't think so.

This is how you can get Buddy to keep 'all four on the floor' when you have visitors:

1. There are a couple of ways you can train Buddy not to jump up at the door. However, by far the most successful one is if you provide a special place for him to sit and greet the guests in a calm manner. A normal-sized mat placed in your entryway will serve the purpose well. The first thing you need to do is, of course, get Buddy to sit and lie down on it so he can get familiar.

2. Place a treat on the mat and get Buddy to come to the entryway. When he notices the treat and comes closer to the mat to eat it, say **"Mat."**

3. Stand a couple of feet away, point to the mat, and say the verbal cue again. Your dog will probably be confused so you might need to throw a treat onto the mat for him to get the idea.

4. Then, after your dog eats the treat, get closer and show him another treat. If he jumps up, whisk the treat away and say **"Oops."** Then, point to the mat and say **"Mat"** again. Wait for Buddy to sit on the mat then mark the behavior and immediately give him the treat.

5. Repeat this for as long as it takes for Buddy to learn that *"Mat"* means *go sit on the mat and wait for your reward there.* Once he starts offering the behavior easily, you can then combine it with a *stay* command to train him to spend some more time on the mat.

6. Then, enlist help from a family member or a friend. Let them knock on the door. When Buddy gets too excited, say **"Mat"** and wait for him to sit there before opening the door. Once you open the door, say **"Stay"** and toss Buddy a

treat. Keep repeating until he understands that he should stay on the mat until the guests have taken off their shoes and coats and are inside the house. Do not forget to praise and reward to encourage the behavior, though.

No Begging, Please

There is nothing more annoying than, when there are friends over for dinner, to have your Bud sitting on the floor, touching every guest with his furry paws, whining and begging to get a slice of that pot roast that smells heavenly. And while that may seem irresistibly cute at first, having your furry friend disrupt your guests after each bite can easily become annoying and may even ruin what was supposed to be a festive meal.

But don't worry. Teaching your dog good table manners is indeed possible. It may take you a while especially if Buddy has been sweeping crumbs from the dinner table for years, but with a good and consistent routine, you can teach your dog to allow you to have your dinner in peace in just a couple of weeks.

Trying the Cold Shoulder

This method is pretty much letting your dog figure out that he is not wanted at the table, on his own:

1. Get everybody on board. Let all of your family members know that they are not supposed to give Buddy food while you are eating, under no circumstances. And this does not only apply to a nice meal at the dining table. You should not feed Buddy even when having a breakfast cereal in the kitchen, or a quick snack on the couch when watching your favorite show.

2. Avoid eye contact, at all costs. When Buddy comes begging for food, simply look away and ignore him completely. By looking at him, you are giving him attention, which in his language means *stay here and whine until I give you a bite of this sandwich.*

3. If he starts begging loudly, say **"Oops."** Then go about your dinner. The point is for him to get the message that he should be excluded from family meals.

4. Don't engage and be patient. Your dog will eventually learn that begging at the table leads to no rewards. Give him a chew toy instead and see if he will be patient. If he doesn't make a fuss about not being allowed to even sweep the morsels, make sure to give him a giant reward once you finish dinner. This will

encourage him to give you your space and wait patiently for his reward.

If the cold shoulder method is taking too long and yields no results, send Buddy to his spot. Just remember, this can contribute to Buddy associating his *spot* with something negative (being excluded from the dinner) if he is overly sensitive. For most dogs though, this works well. Remind Buddy to stay in his spot throughout the dinner. Once you are finished, give him a giant reward. This is really important: give rewards only AFTER you have finished your meal. Otherwise, your dog will probably make the connection that 'begging' leads to '*go to spot*' which leads to 'getting a reward,' which will probably sound like a pretty good deal to him and motivate him to beg some more.

Stop Licking Me... Or Yourself

Licking is one of the most natural behaviors that dogs have. When they are young puppies, their mother licks their skin to show them love, encourage movement, as well as to keep their bodies clean.

They actually explore the world through their tongue, so licking is something they are born to do. But when the licking becomes excessive, it can not only be annoying to watch (as well as hear) but also pretty embarrassing when you are around other people. If Buddy has developed this bad habit, here is how you can put a stop to it:

Tongue Greeting

If Buddy is used to licking your face when he is greeting you, it is because, to him, that is the most natural way to tell you hello. Besides, the human skin is soft which provides comfort for him. Not to mention that it can be salty, which dogs surely find yummy. If that is annoying you (and other people as well), here is how you can get Buddy to forget this bad habit:

1. When you come home from work, if the first thing that Buddy usually does is lick your face, be prepared. Greet him, but just before he is about to stick his tongue out, turn your face away to discourage this habit.

2. The second he retrieves his tongue and withdraws it from your face, mark the behavior, and give him a giant reward to encourage not licking.

3. Repeat this any time he tries to lick greet you. Once Buddy pulls his tongue away, mark, and reward. Eventually, he will get the idea.

What If Buddy Doesn't Give Up?

If Buddy is very persistent and simply doesn't want to pull his tongue away until it touches your skin, you may need to offer him an alternative. See if you can distract him.

1. Turn your face away just like before. If he doesn't seem to give up, use the "*Sit*" command to distract him.

2. Once he sits, tell him that he has been a good boy and give him a reward.

3. Repeat this for as long as it takes for Buddy to get used to having an alternative greeting with you and welcome you calmly, patiently, and with his tongue in his mouth.

Licking His Body

If your dog is licking himself excessively, that can be pretty annoying to watch, as well as hear. Dogs lick their paws to groom and keep them clean, but mostly because it provides them comfort. But, before you start distracting him so he can forget about this annoying habit, it is recommended that you let his vet check him first to rule out underlying conditions. Dogs are known to be wound healers since their saliva speeds up the healing process, so make sure that your Bud is not dealing with a paw injury you are not aware of. If that is not the reason for the excessive licking and is purely a bad habit, then a good distraction technique is in order:

1. Once you notice Buddy is incessantly licking his skin, immediately offer him a proper chew toy or another safe object that will distract him from licking his paws and keep his mind busy.

2. The moment he accepts the toy and starts chewing on it, mark the behavior, and give Buddy a reward.

3. Repeat this for as long as it takes (it might take a while, be patient) for him to associate the excessive licking with chewing on the toy and getting rewarded. He will try to knock down this habit and chew on toys instead, in hopes of getting the treats.

Keep in mind: You cannot replace licking with chewing on toys. Licking is a natural behavior that you cannot (and shouldn't try to) shake your dog out of. Make sure to offer chew toys only when Buddy is licking his skin <u>excessively</u>. Otherwise, it is okay for him to lick.

Stopping Submissive Wetting

Dogs urinate submissively as a way to appease a potential threat. It is an assertive approach of another member of the group who has a much higher rank. This is a mechanism that helps them survive in the dog pack. But what to do when that high-ranking member is you (or another member in your family)? What if your dog is peeing submissively when you enter through the door because he perceives you as a potential threat -someone Buddy feels the need to submit to in such a way?

In order for you to stop submissive urinating, you have to boost Buddy's confidence, as well as keep things low-key:

Boosting His Confidence

Working on building Buddy's confidence, actually means working on stopping the submissive urinating. How? Because in order for Buddy to stop peeing submissively, he first needs to stop perceiving you as a threat. Once Buddy is confident enough to understand that there is no need to feel threatened in any way, the issue will quickly be resolved.

Reward. Keep rewarding your dog whenever he does something right. This is not only important so that Buddy can learn new commands easily, but also because the feeling of getting something right will make him feel more confident in his capabilities.

Distract. When you know that there will be guests coming home, keep Buddy distracted when they arrive. Play a game of fetch or give him some alternative action to perform so that he can act more appropriately around them. Once the surprise moment has passed, and the guests are inside, he will no longer feel the need to urinate submissively. Do this every time to help Buddy act more confidently around new faces.

Give Him a Goal. At the heart of submissive wetting is a pet that simply wants to please his owner. You need to make sure that Buddy has a goal to achieve for most of the day so that he will not feel the need to urinate as much around you. Maintaining a regular training routine, chewing on toys, going on longer walks, and just keeping him active, will help you achieve that.

Avoiding Drama

Submissive urinating is really not hard to solve. All you need to do to grow Buddy out of this habit is to keep greeting low key and avoid the departure-arrival drama:

1. When you enter through the door, do not pay any attention to Buddy. Do NOT approach him by any means, give him time and let him come to you instead.

2. Greet him without making eye contact. Instead, offer him your palm. This is really important as the palm of your hand transmits only positive energy, while the back of the hand is associated with negative behavior.

3. Let Buddy sniff your hand and do not say a word.

4. Then, pat him under his chin, <u>never</u> on top of the head as that only encourages submissive behavior.

5. Do not reach for your dog and never grab him until he stops being submissive, that is.

6. Keep everyone informed. When you have guests coming over, let them know about your issue and tell them to ignore Buddy as well. Your submissive dog should be given the time to get comfortable on his own. Tell your guests to avoid making eye contact and to let Buddy come to them.

7. Follow these steps for as long as it takes for Buddy to stop wetting submissively around people.

<u>NEVER</u> punish your dog for urinating submissively. Do not yell at him, and by all means, do not get angry. That will only have a counter effect. If your dog notices that you are angry, he will be encouraged to urinate some more. If that makes you even angrier, then Buddy will pee some more. As long as you show anger and dissatisfaction, your dog will get more and more submissive as his response will be to desperately try to turn off that anger.

Fun Games for Practice and Bonding

If you know someone who has a well-trained dog, then chances are, they've already managed to impress you with a trick or two. And while it may seem that teaching your dog these fun games is almost impossible, the truth is, most dogs master them even quicker than other commands. That is because the dog is already trained and has adopted proper habits. So if you were thinking about skipping this chapter because, in your opinion, Buddy couldn't possibly master them, let me convince you otherwise.

The key to teaching these games and tricks is in the *sequencing*. That means that, when trying to teach a new trick to your dog, you need to break it into small components that will be easy for him to master, which will, of course, add up to him learning the whole trick.

Now, get ready to wow your friends and family with these astonishing tricks and games you can play with Buddy:

High-Five

High-Five is probably the most popular trick that you can teach your dog. The goal here is, obviously, to get Buddy to raise one of his paws as high as possible. That can be taught in four sequences:

Sequence 1

1. Sit on the floor and have Buddy in front of you.

2. Make sure to reduce your posture either by squatting in front of Buddy or by kneeling, so that you can ensure that

you are not hovering or even leaning over your dog.

3. Place your palm somewhere in the mid-chest area, offer it to Buddy, and say **"Shake,"** or whatever verbal cue you wish to use.

4. Lift his dominant front leg off the floor a couple of inches by taking it with your other hand.

5. Then, slide your hand that you offered to him, down to his paw and give Buddy a gentle shake. As you start shaking his hand, praise him enthusiastically to show him how positive and exciting it is to shake hands.

6. Then, give your dog a treat as a reward and give him the release cue.

7. Do five repetitions over three sessions to help Buddy learn the *shake hands* command.

Sequence 2

1. Sit in front of your dog and, again, reduce your posture to make sure you're not leaning or hovering over him.

2. Offer your palm and give him the *Shake* command. Wait for Buddy's response. If he is not willingly offering this behavior, touch his elbow to remind him what he has to do, and then offer the palm again. Make sure to give Buddy a chance to lift the paw on his own.

3. Once he lifts his paw, take it, then praise, reward, and release.

4. If Buddy is not giving his paw on command, then take it yourself, but praise and reward again.

5. Repeat this for as long as it takes for him to start lifting it on cue.

Sequence 3

1. Just like before, sit in front of Buddy and reduce the posture of your body.

2. Offer him your palm and give the "*Shake*" command. At this point, Buddy should put the paw in your palm, willingly.

3. Praise, reward, and release.

4. If he is not giving you his paw, then you are probably moving too fast. Go back to Sequence 2 and repeat some more.

Sequence 4

1. Sit in front of Buddy with a reduced posture.

2. Offer him the palm and give the "*Shake*" command. Your dog should willingly put the paw into your palm. If not, go back to Sequence 3 and repeat some more.

3. Now, raise your palm as high as your dog can possibly place it. Try doing it in 2-inch increments. Do this about a dozen times, and you will notice how your dog will stretch his paw willingly, each time.

4. Do not forget to praise, reward, and then release.

Roll Over

Just like high-five, rollover is also one of the most popular tricks for the whole family to play with their furry member. For this trick, your dog needs to lic on the floor and then roll over sideways. Of course, Buddy needs to have mastered the *down* command first. If your dog has managed to learn that and responds well to treats, then you will have no problem in helping him master this trick as well.

1. Instruct Buddy to get into the *Down position*.

2. Kneel down in front of your dog, making sure that you are not leaning over him.

3. Have an irresistible treat in your hand and hold it in a way that Buddy will have to look at it over his shoulders.

4. Say **"Roll Over"** and immediately make a gentle circle with the treat hand over his head, making sure that you keep the treat close to his nose the whole time.

5. With the other hand, physically get your dog started in making the *roll* by gently

pushing him in the direction that you want him to go.

6. Once your dog has rolled over completely, immediately praise and reward him. Repeat for as long as it takes for Buddy to become relaxed when you are rolling him over.

Sequence 2

1. Instruct Buddy to *lie down* and kneel in front of him.

2. Have a tasty treat in your hand.

3. Say **"Roll Over"** and make a circle with the treat head over his nose. This time, do not help Buddy to roll over with your other hand.

4. If Buddy Rolls over on his own, praise and reward immediately. If not, go back to Sequence 1 and practice some more.

5. Repeat until Buddy is really comfortable and performs the behavior with minimum guidance.

Sequence 3

1. Get Buddy to *lie down* and sit in front of him.

2. Say **"Roll Over"** but this time, do not show him the treat.

3. If Buddy rolls over on cue, your job is almost done. Just practice this some more, until he becomes more relaxed in his position. If not, go back to the previous sequence.

4. Do not forget to praise and reward.

Tug

Who doesn't like to have a well-behaved dog they can play *tug* with? And while you may have heard stories that playing *tug* increases the chances for your dog to show aggressive and dominant behavior, that is simply not true. Playing *tug* with your dog can be quite beneficial actually, as it teaches him to defer to you as well as training him to channel his urges better and to control himself.

Buy a knotted rope for this purpose, and follow these steps:

1. Bring out the rope and play with it for a while. Throw it, shake it, do whatever it takes for it to get Buddy excited.

2. Once Buddy approaches you and grabs it, pull gently on the rope to motivate him to show resistance.

3. Once he does that, say **"Good Boy," and tug.**

4. Then, get even more energetic with the tugging.

5. After about 10 seconds, stop, and give your dog the *Give* command.

6. Once he lets go of the rope, mark the good behavior and then reward.

7. If Buddy refuses to give you the rope, trick him by placing a yummy treat on the floor. Then take the rope away from him.

8. Then, try the *tug* game again. Repeat until you get Buddy to *give* you the rope.

Remember that you should be the one who will win most of the times. However, it is okay to let Buddy win occasionally. Just make sure that, after you are done playing, you put the rope away, as Buddy needs to know that the knotted rope is for playing *tug* only.

Play Dead

This trick is a real crowd-pleaser. It consists of you holding an invisible gun and giving Buddy a *Bang!* So he can roll on his side and play dead. Sounds like too good to pass on? Follow these steps and teach Buddy this super fun trick:

Sequence 1

1. Get Buddy in a "*Down*" position. Hold a treat in your 'gun' hand.

2. Then, lean over your dog, and say **"Bang"** in a firm voice, while pointing your index finger at Buddy. Here, Buddy is supposed to roll on his back or his side.

3. If he does that, mark the behavior and the reward him like crazy. If not, then you should use the treat as you did for

the *"Roll Over"* trick to get him to roll on his side.

4. Praise, reward, and then release.

5. Repeat for as long as it takes for Buddy to starts reacting on the *"Bang"* command.

Sequence 2

1. The goal here is to get Buddy to play dead even from a standing or sitting position, without instructing him to get *"down"* first. To do so, get your dog's attention first.

2. Then, lean over him and give him the *"Bang"* command as you point the finger at him. If Buddy is a quick learner, he will lie down, roll over, and play dead. If that happens, mark the behavior immediately, then reward, and release.

3. If he doesn't get what you are asking him to do, put him in the "*down*" position physically, and then trick him to roll over, to show him what you mean. Again, mark, reward, and release.

Sequence 3

1. Now, let's try doing it at a distance. Stand about 2 feet from Buddy, and get his attention.

2. Use the "*Bang*" command and 'shoot' him with your index finger.

3. If Buddy responds, praise, reward, release. If not, show him what is asked of him and start over.

4. Once Buddy gets the point, start increasing the distance gradually until you are 6 feet apart from each other.

Belly Crawl

Another fun game is to get Buddy to crawl on his belly. To do so, perform the following steps:

1. Stand in front of your dog and get him in the "*Down"* position.

2. Hold a treat in front of his nose, but make sure that he cannot grab it.

3. With the treat about 1-2 inches off the ground, slowly make a step back, and very carefully and slowly, move the treat toward you.

4. The point here is for Buddy to start dragging his body forward in order to follow the treat.

5. Once you notice your dog doing that, mark the behavior instantly, and give him the treat.

6. Keep repeating this exercise, allowing Buddy to crawl further and further forward.

7. Once Buddy is comfortable with the exercise, you can fade out the treat and do this in either a hand motion or by teaching a *Crawl* verbal cue. Just say **"Crawl"** every time Buddy starts dragging himself to follow the treat, and he will quickly associate the cue with the dragging behavior.

Take a Bow

Wouldn't it be nice if your dog could "*take a bow*" after performing some of the previous tricks for a friend of yours? Now that would be a real cherry on the top of the cake, wouldn't it? Fortunately, teaching Buddy to take a bow is no more complicated than the previous games. Just make sure that he has already mastered the *"Stand"* and *"Down"* command, and you are good to go:

Sequence 1

1. Get Buddy to stand near you, at a *Heel* position.

2. Place your left palm under Buddy's belly and against the hind legs, apply slight backward pressure.

3. Slide your right hand through his collar and place it under the chin.

4. Then, say **"Take a Bow"** while applying a slight downward pressure there.

5. The point here is for Buddy to be standing on his rear end and lower the front. If he struggles to perform this, see if you can lower his front end with the use of a treat lure.

6. Once he succeeds, mark, reward, and release.

7. Repeat for as long as it takes for him to become comfortable in doing this on his own.

Sequence 2

1. Instruct Buddy to get into a *"Stand"* position. Make sure to keep your left hand under the belly.

2. Say **"Take a Bow"** and gently pat the ground with your other hand, to encourage him.

3. Once he lowers the front end, mark the behavior immediately and give him a reward. Release.

Sequence 3

1. Now, it is time for Buddy to do it on cue. Instruct him to get in a *"Stand"* position.

2. Point to the ground with your right hand, and say **"Take a Bow."**

3. When he does as asked, praise, reward, and release. If he wants to get "*down*," you can use your left hand to gently prop up the rear end.

4. Repeat this for as long as it takes for Buddy to be able to do it on command, without you propping the rear end.

5. When he finally gets the point and takes a bow, give him the "*Stay*" command to hold that position. After a couple of seconds, release.

6. Make sure to praise, and reward, and be ready for some applause.

Phasing Out the Treats

Now that you have instilled discipline and managed to teach good manners and basic commands to your furry friend, you probably wonder how much longer you will be dependent on the stinky treats.

You have been using yummy doggy treats in two ways:

1) To lure your dog into performing a behavior that he otherwise doesn't want to or doesn't know how to perform.

2) To reward your Bud after he has willingly responded in a positive way to your command.

And as much as the treats seem like the most useful training tool (which is in most cases true), they provide your dog with neither relevant nor valuable life rewards. Once you start integrating consistent training into Buddy's life, you will need to start phasing out the treats progressively.

The Food Lures

The first stages of training are comprised of the substitution of the food lures with hand signals and verbal commands. The goal of each command is to use the verbal cue as a lure for your dog to perform the desired behavior.

If Buddy is stubborn and you are still quite dependent on using treats to get his body in a certain position, then the first step you need to do is to replace the food lures with *hand signals.*

In order for you to use the hand signals right, Buddy shouldn't be distracted. So hide the stinky treats in your pockets, and with an empty hand, try to show him what you want him to do. For instance, if you are struggling to get Buddy to sit down and you previously used a treat to get him into a sitting position, you can now do the same thing, only with an empty hand. Your Bud has been following the movement of your hand for so long, that he will probably continue doing so even if you are not holding a treat. Give this a try. If Buddy sits down, mark the behavior, and give him a treat as a reward.

You can also practice this around <u>dinner time.</u> Prepare Buddy's dinner and place his food bowl on the counter. Then give Buddy the verbal command and hand signal for "*Sit*." If he complies, give him a piece of kibble. If not, take the bowl away. It is pretty simple really: sit and have dinner or refuse to sit down and don't get your bowl. That way, Buddy will be given a chance to catch on quickly, which you can later use for all commands.

The Food Rewards

Eventually, you will want to fade out the food rewards as giving him a piece of sausage every time he sits down is not only inconvenient but will also cause treat dependency. There are a couple of ways or different stages when it comes to phasing out the treat rewards:

Longer Sequences

Whereas a treat at the beginning of the training is definitely needed when your dog manages to lie down, surely it is unnecessary for each subsequent session? Besides, it can also be ineffective as you want your Bud to improve during following training sessions, not to make a huge deal for performing the simplest command that he has already known for a couple of weeks. Look at it this way – you would applaud a 5-year-old for learning how to spell his name, but you surely wouldn't think that a 15-year old deserves a reward for performing the same action.

Once you are sure that your dog knows how to perform a certain behavior, the next time, ask him for a little extra in order to earn the reward. As Buddy's training progresses, increase the length of the sequences for a single reward.

Delay the Reward

In addition, you should also increase the length of the time it takes you to give Buddy the reward after performing the desired behavior. Don't be so quick to fill his mouth with irresistible freeze-dried liver just because he has been a good boy. If you are sure that Buddy has already mastered a particular command, prolong the treat. Keep in mind that the longer you delay giving Buddy the food reward, the more focused he will be on you.

After delaying the reward, you can try asking for several responses for a single reward. In this case, obviously, you should plan to give the reward after the performance of the trickier, more complex behavior.

Other Rewards

Once Buddy can perform several responses for a single reward, it is time to say farewell to the food reward, completely. Think of replacing the yummy treats with fun games, petting, a nice walk, or simply by rewarding him with something else he likes to do.

Phasing out the rewards is extremely important because, after a while, your dog may even stop responding to them. Food rewards are great in the initial stages of training, but in real life, they may be overshadowed by other more interesting things. No dog would choose to sit down and get a reward when he can run and play with other canine companions in the park. The latter seems much more fun, don't you think? That is why the best way to maintain good behavior is to replace the food rewards with some things your dog enjoys more.

Addressing Anxiety Correctly

Dogs are social animals. It is in their genes to have relationships with other dogs from their pack. And that's what we love most about dogs – the fact that we can create a strong social bond with them. After all, that's why we call them man's best friend.

But as much as they love spending time with us, their emotions are even more intense when, all of a sudden, they are found alone in the house. This condition is called *separation anxiety*. It is the emotional response to being separated from the human (or humans) that the dog is attached to the most.

Unfortunately, this condition is not uncommon and is particularly present among rescue dogs. But even though pretty much everyone is aware of it, dog owners usually make the situation worse. How? In hopes to somehow make the dog feel better, they make a big fuss about their departure, which only leaves Buddy feeling more alone. When separation anxiety strikes, it is really important to address it the right way if you want to improve Buddy's emotional health.

Recognize It On Time

Although the root cause is the same, no dog goes through separation anxiety the same way. This emotional condition can take various forms and affect your furry friend with different intensities. Recognizing this condition in Buddy can not only help you address it the right way and improve his mental wellbeing, but it will also contribute to more successful training results, as well.

Here are some of the signs that indicate that your dog is suffering from separation anxiety:

- Follows you around the house when you leave the room, regardless of how briefly you are gone

- When you get ready to leave the house, Buddy is whining, shaking, crying, or panting

- Chewing objects around the house when left alone

- Eliminating waste inside the house when left alone

- Scratching the doors and walls and digging at the floor when left alone

- Neighbors complain about loud and constant barking when you are not at home

Counter Condition It

In theory, counter conditioning a dog means training him to start associating something that he is afraid of with a reward. When the dog is suffering from separation anxiety, the fearful thing here is being separated from your or another family member. To counter condition it, you will have to provide something rewarding in return. Buddy has to associate your departure with something that he really enjoys. And what are the things that dogs love most (besides spending time with you)? Food and toys, of course.

For counter conditioning, think of giving your dog a toy stuffed with yummy treats. Just before you leave the house, give your dog a puzzle toy stuffed with crunchy biscuits, pieces of sausage, freeze-dried liver, and other yummy doggy treats. Another great thing is to also spread the inside of the puzzle with some low-fat peanut butter to keep Buddy busy longer. The goal here is to keep Buddy busy for at least half an hour, which should be enough for him to forget the fact that he was afraid of being left alone.

When you get back home, remove the puzzle toy, and keep it out of his sight. The whole point is for Buddy to be conditioned to being able to have it only when you are not at home.

Make sure not to give Buddy the puzzle toy at other times in order for it to be rewarding. If Buddy is given access to it on other occasions as well, it might not be enough to compensate for the sad feeling when you leave the house.

Desensitize Buddy to Solitude

Keep in mind that there isn't a quick cure that can help your Bud grow out of separation anxiety. If his condition is mild to severe, be realistic and do not expect him to get cured overnight. Another way that can help your dog to knock down the intensity of this condition, is to gradually get him used to being left alone.

And the best way to do that is to desensitize him to solitude and help him understand that the fact that you are leaving the house does not equal abandonment.

Keep in mind that this is a process that will most likely take a few weeks, and requires a great deal of patience and consistency. However, it has proven to be super effective and can have positive results in the long haul.

1. The first thing you need to do is to actually work on Buddy's feelings associated with your pre-departure. It is recommended that you gradually get him used to these actions. This is best achieved if you engage in these actions throughout the day without actually leaving the house so that your dog can start perceiving them as less scary. For instance, put on your coat and shoes and walk around your home for some

time, then take them off. Take the car keys and jiggle them a couple of minutes, then put them back. Do the same things you do before you leave for work, without actually leaving the house.

2. Work on getting Buddy more used to having you out of his sight by spending more time in another room. Doing this every day should eventually make him feel less alone when you actually leave the house.

3. Once he becomes comfortable with you being out of his sight, try blocking his access to you, for instance, by closing the door. Gradually increase the time your dog spends without having access to you. Just make sure that these out-of-sight stays are in the bathroom or in another room, and not actually out of

the house, as this may be too stressful for him at this moment.

4. Do this practice for at least 2-3 weeks before actually going out the door. However, if you have an alternate door you can use, such as a back door, or a garage door, that would be much better. Stay there for a minute or two, then 5, then 10, and gradually increase the amount of time you are out.

5. As you begin increasing the time, you should also start incorporating the puzzle toy here, in order to keep Buddy busy.

Be Patient

Keep in mind that it will take a long time before your dog becomes comfortable with the prolonged time alone. For most dogs, the undesirable and destructive behavior kicks in the first 30-40 minutes after the departure. However, it can take a while before you can actually leave Buddy alone for 40 minutes, comfortably.

Once you manage to leave your dog alone for 60 to 90 minutes, then Buddy is surely able to handle 4-6 hours of solitude. But, even then, see if you can leave him alone for shorter periods of time. If you have a friend or a neighbor that can help you out with this, it can make a huge difference as most dogs are anxious when left completely alone, not when their owner is out of their sight.

Don't Be Afraid to Seek Assistance

If you have tried everything in your power to make Buddy comfortable with being left alone, from crate training to counter conditioning and desensitizing, and yet, he is still shaking when you get ready to leave the house and cannot bear being left alone, then it is probably time to seek help from a CPDT (Certified Professional Dog Trainer). Ask your vet to recommend one to you, or search the internet and find one in your area. A CPDT will surely be able to help you solve the issue and address your dog's condition in a more personalized manner.

Bonus Chapter: Agility Training

Agility training is a competitive but extremely fun doggy sport. The agility course is obstacle-made, and it consists of jumps, walkways, tunnels, and all sorts of interesting things that dogs really love. But, besides doing it for fun or competition, agility training your dog will strengthen your bond, and most importantly, keep him fit, healthy, and in perfect shape.

Because the whole point of the sport is trying to overcome the obstacles mostly by jumping, it is not recommended for young dogs and puppies. The best time for you to introduce agility training to Buddy is between the first and second year of his life.

There are a lot of fun agility training methods and techniques that you can teach Buddy. Here are the best ones to start with in order to help your Bud fall in love with this fun sport:

Tunnels

Tunnels are probably the easiest obstacle to teach, so it is recommended to introduce them first. However, don't go in over your head. Keep in mind that you are teaching Buddy something new; something that probably looks scary to him. You cannot expect him to go through super long tunnels. Start with a short tunnel where Buddy can see through to the other side. Have a friend stand on the other side of the tunnel, waiting for him with his favorite toy. You can even coax him to get inside by placing a couple of yummy treats inside.

Don't forget to praise and reward Buddy when he finally makes it through. Once he becomes more comfortable, you can introduce longer or even curved tunnels.

Contact Obstacles

Contact obstacles are obstacles that have specific ends that Buddy will have to touch with his paws. There are a few contact obstacles that you have to try:

The Dog Walk – Which is a balance beam that has ramps on each end.

The A-Frame – A walkway in the shape of a cone where dogs have to walk up the incline and then come down the other side.

The Teether-Totter – Which is just like a regular one. The board will move under the dog's weight while your furry friend tries to walk across the obstacle.

To teach Buddy how to make the contact, you can start by placing treats at the ends of the obstacles. Just make sure that you start from the lowest possible position so your dog will be comfortable.

However, if Buddy is scared or refuses to go, you can try introducing them in reverse. Pick up Buddy and place him at one end so that he can take a step to take off. As he gets more comfortable, place him further and further up to make it more challenging.

Weave Poles

Weave poles are poles that Buddy will have to weave in and out of in order to succeed. This is a somewhat more challenging obstacle, so don't expect quick results and have a lot of patience.

Most trainers suggest clipping wires onto the poles to create a path that the dog can follow. First, place the poles about shoulder-width apart from Buddy and at his head's level so he cannot go under or over them. Throw a few treats onto the path to encourage him to start walking. Once he takes a step forward, praise him like crazy. As he gets comfortable, lift up the wires gradually until he can weave easily without them.

Regular Jumps

If your vet gives you the green light and says that Buddy's joints are in perfect shape, you can then introduce the jumps. However, don't start off high. If Buddy is of a small breed, place the bar on the ground. If he is of a medium breed, place the bar one inch off the ground. If he is a large dog, start with the bar only 2 inches off the ground.

To teach Buddy to jump, make sure he is leashed to avoid him having to go around the hurdle. Give specific commands for each jump, and remember to praise and reward him when he succeeds.

If Buddy is afraid to jump, practice this in a narrow hallway. Place something that blocks his way completely, and stay on the other side.

Show Buddy a treat and call him to you enthusiastically. Since Buddy will have no other way but over the obstacle, eventually he will make the jump. Again, make sure not to place it too high off the ground. Praise and reward.

Tire Jumps

Start with the tire placed on the ground. Enlist a friend or a family member to hold the tire for you. Tap the tire gently to encourage your dog to go through. You can also coax him to start moving by placing some yummy treats. Let your Buddy just walk through it first. Praise and reward the good boy. Then, lift it off the ground a bit. Keep increasing the height gradually, until your dog has to jump through it. Once he does that, praise him like crazy and give him a really big treat.

Start Sequencing

Once Buddy gets comfortable with overcoming these obstacles, you can start combining them together for better results. Start by combing only two obstacles, such as the tunnels and a teeter-totter, then work your way up until Buddy has no problem in completing the whole course. When he becomes really comfortable, then you can start considering competing for real.

Conclusion

People often say that their dogs are not listening to them. But in fact, it is not so much that their furry friends don't listen, but that they don't understand what their owners are trying to tell them. I hope that this book was able to help you teach verbal cues to your dog and that you have also managed to become a bit more fluent in doggish as well.

With the information in this book, you should be able to teach Buddy basic commands as well as to take him for long walks calmly, in less than a month. Just remember, dog training is not something that you teach overnight, but a skill that should be practiced regularly in order to maintain good behavior and encourage proper discipline.

I hope that I was able to help you tame naughty Buddy, and I wish you both a long and lasting human-canine bond!

www.ingramcontent.com/pod-product-compliance
Lightning Source LLC
Chambersburg PA
CBHW071236070526
44583CB00017B/2212